CHANGE MAKERS

Make your mark with more impact and less drama

Roz —
Don't go changing!

Enjoy 😊

Digby

DIGBY SCOTT

DIGBY SCOTT

CHANGE MAKERS

Make your mark with more impact and less drama

d

Paperback: ISBN 978-0-473-47096-8

Kindle: ISBN 978-0-473-47097-5

PDF: ISBN 978-0-473-47098-2

iBook: ISBN 978-0-473-47099-9

EPUB: 978-0-473-47446-1

Every effort has been made to trace (and seek permission for use of) the original source material used within this book. Where the attempt has been unsuccessful, the publisher would be pleased to hear from the author/publisher to rectify any omission.

A catalogue record for this book is available from the National Library of New Zealand.

Published by Digby Scott

Edited by Clear Edit NZ

Cover and text design by Louise Horner

Printed and bound in New Zealand by Yourbooks.co.nz

To all aspiring
Change Makers
everywhere.

CONTENTS

INTRODUCTION

ARE YOU RESTLESS?

Are you ready to make an impact? Are you really ready? Good. Let's begin.

To start with, let me remind you of something.

You cannot *not* make an impact.

You can't argue with that, right? I first heard it when I attended training in neuro-linguistic programming years ago, and it's stuck with me ever since.

Whenever you show up, you have an impact, whether you consciously intend to or not. Even your silence, or your absence, has an impact. The mere fact that you exist causes ripples. Those ripples land somewhere. And they have some sort of impact.

Remember that.

You're probably going to impact 10,000 people in your life. The question is: What kind of impact do you want to have? The opportunity is there to make our lives extraordinary through our work.

What sort of mark do you want to make?

Drew Dudley gave a short and brilliant talk about this when he spoke at the TED conference about Everyday Leadership. His idea was that our words and actions can have a profound and lasting impact, and often we don't even realise it. They have a ripple effect. The thing is, we don't know where or how the ripples will land. We can forget what we did or said until someone tells us about the powerful effect we had on them.

So, it's good to be mindful of what we're saying and doing.

But why be content with ripples? Why not create bow waves? If we only have a certain number of years on the planet, we might as well put them to good use, right?

RESTLESS GO-GETTERS

This book is for restless go-getters who want to create bow waves rather than merely ripples. Is that you? Deep down, I think you'll find that it is.

If you're asking any of these questions:

- How can I change how stuff gets done around here?
- How can I stay true to myself amidst the chaos?
- How can I learn to say no?
- How do I get traction and make my mark in this new role?
- How do I ensure I don't get stuck in the weeds, and keep a broader perspective?
- Where am I going in my career? How can I find the role or place that's 'me'?
- How can I reshape myself as an influential leader, not simply a technical expert?

...then this book is for you.

Or, if you're thinking any of these thoughts:

- I'm so frustrated right now. I feel like I'm going around in circles.
- I can see what needs to be done, but it's scary. I might fail.
- I feel like an imposter. Who am I to make this happen?
- If I want to be credible, I've got to show my expertise. Otherwise I'm a fake.
- It's not safe for me to be vulnerable or show my true colours in this culture/environment.
- Making change is too hard. It's easier to keep my head down and play it safe.

...then this book is definitely for you.

You're not alone. In the quiet conversations with trusted friends, in the journals of aspiring Change Makers, in the thousands of one-on-one coaching conversations I've been privileged to be a part of over the past 20 years or so, these are the sorts of challenges leaders, and aspiring leaders, face every day. I've heard them enough times that I wanted to write this book to help you navigate the task of making change happen with less unnecessary friction and more fun, both for yourself and for the world you live and work in.

But wait. Aren't we supposed to be fearless leaders who have this stuff sorted? Haven't we been hired because we're on top of our game? The fact is, we all go through this stuff, all the time. You're in good company. Welcome.

MAKE SOME WAVES

This book is your guide to help you face down those questions and thoughts. You want to thrive in the face of change, and make a real difference, right? That's what this book is about. It will help you to:

- Get (back) in touch with what you stand for.
- Find your voice.
- Take your ideas from inspiration to implementation.
- Build the relationships that help you grow and get stuff done.
- Take the critical actions that keep you moving forward, however scary that may be.
- Make change happen and make your mark with less stress and more grace.

"There's no safe way to be great."

BOB ANDERSON, AUTHOR OF *MASTERING LEADERSHIP*

This book is for restless go-getters (you) who are looking for inspiration, strategies, and practical ideas to make the difference they want to make in the world. The book centres on how you can develop four qualities to help you: Conviction, Curiosity, Connection, and Courage. The idea being that if you have these in spades, you can more easily have the impact you want to make, and live a richer, more interesting, and more rewarding life.

It's also a book about stepping away from safety. To lead a full and rich life, and to lead others genuinely and effectively, you need to cross a threshold. Beyond the threshold, you're asked to dial down the need to be certain, right, and safe. And you'll need to dial up your willingness and ability to be a voracious learner, and to be vulnerable, authentic, and bold.

In my experience as a business leader and as a leadership development practitioner who's worked with hundreds of organisations and thousands of managers, I believe a majority of people sit on the edge of this threshold. They're poised for greatness, but they're stuck. They need that supportive, yet firm, nudge to tip them over so they can fly. In a volatile, unpredictable world, it's easy to cling to safety. But, as Bob Anderson, author of *Mastering Leadership*, says, "There's no safe way to be great." The world needs more purposeful, bold, restless go-getters. And this book is that nudge. You'll find plenty of practical tools and tips on how to step across the threshold, as well as stories of others who have done the same.

So, if you have a burning desire to have a more meaningful impact, but you're playing a little safer than you need to be, keep reading. If you're trying to make change happen, but feel like you're going around in circles, keep reading. This book is about going beyond the threshold of safety and sameness, into a world where you consistently make the impact you want to make, and have fun while you're doing it. Let's get on with it. Let's go make some waves.

INTRODUCING YOUR GUIDE

Let me introduce myself. It's worthwhile knowing a bit about the person who's going to be taking you on this journey.

In 1992 I was a bored chartered accountant who was responsible for auditing big publicly listed companies. I felt that there had to be more to life than this, and had an inner drive to go and discover more. So I left the safety of accounting and set off on an adventure to see what was possible.

Over the coming years I worked all over the world. I ran a ski rental shop, slaved as a commercial salmon fisherman, taught windsurfing, went busking with my favourite guitar, grew my hair out, embraced the nineties, and got that earring (which I was incredibly proud of at the time).

Eventually I realised I needed to re-engage my brain and ended up in London working for a major recruitment company getting jobs for accountants in big investment banks.

I ran away wanting adventure, to buck the system, to find out what's possible, but then I ended up working back in the same big old corporate system again.

After a couple of years and realising that London wasn't my long-term game, I set off on more travel and eventually landed in New Zealand. I was offered the opportunity to become the National Manager for a multi-national recruitment company and my ego said, "YES!" Being relatively inexperienced and without a lot of support, I ended up burning out big time after only a couple of years.

This led me to an early mid-life crisis at the age of 30 where I was forced to really examine what I was about and what I really wanted out of life. That period of introspection and exploration led me on the path that I'm still on today, 20 years later.

I thought I could only have one or the other:

1. Be the **Rebel** – the untamed lone wolf, true to myself, an individual thinker so I could buck the system, or

2. Be the **Prefect** – be responsible, agree to the rules of the game, be a team player and become part of the system so I could influence it.

What I've learned is that fusing our inner rebel and inner prefect together is what creates effective, adaptable leaders who are able to create and ride the next wave of change, and continually rise to every occasion.

Over the last 20 years I've seen how deliberately cultivating a bold, adaptable nature from these two fused parts has completely transformed my restless go-getting clients, allowing them to thrive.

AS CHANGE MAKERS AND LEADERS WE GET TO CHOOSE OUR FUTURES.

Do we shrink back and play it safe, or do we learn how to adapt, lean into discomfort and rise above, paving the way for our people to do the same? That is the question central to my life, and to this book.

Part One:

THE WORLD NEEDS YOUR VOICE

CHAPTER ONE: CROSSING THE THRESHOLD

THE WAITING GAME

Always this energy smoulders inside, when it remains unlit, the body fills with dense smoke.

DAVID WHYTE, 'Out on the Ocean'

I once found myself as a director and part-owner of a successful consultancy firm. I was busy, but not happy. I joined the firm because, as a successful leadership development practitioner, I wanted to see if I could grow a leveraged business, having others do the 'practitioner' work. The first couple of years were fun, but I increasingly lost my mojo as time went on. The management work seemed increasingly tedious, and I missed being a practitioner. I missed being at the cutting edge of thought-leadership, teaching, and working directly with leaders on their vexing issues. I missed seeing the sparkle in their eyes when we found a breakthrough. I grew increasingly disengaged with the business. And I kept on showing up. I told myself, "Just get over yourself, and keep on fitting in." Truth be told, as a director and part owner, I felt a huge responsibility to stay on and play my part in making the business succeed. And the future outside was unclear. I was waiting for change to happen, and I was stuck.

Sometime during that period, a wise friend said to me, "You're like a horse running around in a paddock that's too small for you!" Those words spoke the truth to me, and they jarred. I heard the dulcet whispers of Winston Churchill in my ears:

Men occasionally stumble over the truth, but most of them pick themselves up and hurry off as if nothing ever happened.

Well, I didn't 'hurry off'. That conversation was the turning point for me. It was the start of an exciting, yet extremely challenging period. I started to step up to and cross a threshold. I began to re-claim my voice. I began a new journey of making my mark in the world in the way that I truly wanted to.

This book is about how you can do that too.

PLAYING IT SAFE

Do you want to make an impact, but know you're playing it a little safe? Are you feeling restless and frustrated with your work, your talents under-utilised? Is something 'out of alignment'? Do you want to make a bigger difference that reflects what you really stand for?

If so, you're not alone. It's a familiar story, right? The talented individual wants to make a dent in the universe, and at the same time they're being tentative and playing it too safe.

My guess is that you're probably really good at what you do. You've had success. You might be wondering what's next. Perhaps you're a little restless.

And...

Maybe you're holding back on going for it. Maybe you're waiting until things get easier. Maybe waiting for the right time. Telling yourself it's not really possible to create what you'd love to create.

I've been there. Sometimes I still go there. It's a crappy place to be.

Don't beat yourself up too much though. Making change happen is hard. Here are some reasons why:

- **You're going against the rules.**
  In a study conducted by the global pharmaceutical company Merck, 84% of workers reported that their employers encouraged curiosity, but 60% say they encounter practical barriers to it. Rules, processes, and procedures all exist to ensure we don't stuff things up. They don't do a lot to help us create the new.

- **You're going against the grain.**
  Harvard Professor Francesca Gino, author of *Rebel Talent*, conducted a survey of over 2000 employees. Nearly half the respondents reported working in organisations where they regularly feel the need to conform, and more than half said that people in their organisations do not question the status quo.

- **You're going against the brain.**
  Neuroscience tells us that our brains are wired to seek certainty. Leading adult development psychologists such as Bill Torbert and Robert Kegan tell us that most of us primarily operate from a 'fear-based' mindset, where the focus is on avoiding bad things from happening, rather than bringing a worthwhile vision into being.

No wonder it's easier to play it safe!

INTERESTING TIMES

May you live in interesting times.
May you live in an interesting age.
May you live in exciting times.

ANON

This phrase purportedly originated in China hundreds of years ago. While the source is debatable, the sentiment is relevant. It's fair to say that we're living through interesting times right now.

Robert Kennedy, back in 1966, said:

Like it or not, we live in interesting times. They are times of danger and uncertainty, but they are also more open to the creative energy of men than any other time in history.

He could have been speaking today. Think about what he's saying. "...more open to the creative energy..." Kennedy is inviting us to step up and grasp the opportunity that these interesting times give us.

We live in a 'great unfreezing', kind of like the end of the last ice age. Models and assumptions that have run our lives for hundreds of years are being challenged and melting away. While this can be scary, it's also a time of great opportunity.

Here are just a few areas of our global society facing significant upheavals and challenges that make for interesting times:

- **Employment models**
  The 'permanent job' is increasingly a myth. Careers are fluid. Talented people are increasingly choosing how and where to spend their time and energy. How we organise to get work done is changing. Lifelong learning is essential to thrive.

- **Business models**
  Age-old business models are being challenged and eroded in all quarters. What we thought of as rock solid has proven to be soluble. Think of the accommodation industry, taxis, insurance, even how we buy and sell physical goods. It's all changing.

- **Capitalism**
  The capitalist model has helped to lift world living standards massively over the 20th century. And we're experiencing the significant downsides of that. The World Economic Forum's 2018 global risks report highlights rising income and wealth disparity as one of the key trends driving profound social instability.

Interesting times ask us to be at our best.

They challenge our assumptions and boundaries and ask us to look beyond them. They ask us what we really stand for. They ask us to invent new ways of seeing and living in the world. They invite us to take a stand for something. The challenge for each of us is to step up to those challenges and create a way through.

And therein lies the problem. Not enough of us are adept to thrive in interesting times.

Here's an analogy. Most computer operating systems have a 'safe mode', which a user can boot into when there's a problem with the system. Safe mode is designed to keep the integrity of the system stable and intact while making the problem go away. It's designed for maintenance, not functionality. It's a defensive approach that focuses on restoring the status quo when the system can't handle what's thrown at it.

Interesting times throw gnarly problems at us that can cause us to go into 'safe mode'. When something unfamiliar shows up, we can put up our defences and play it safe. We batten down the hatches, try to maintain some sort of equilibrium, and endeavour to make the problems go away. But like a computer operating system, all we're doing is putting energy into maintenance, and not tapping all of our functional design as human beings. What a waste!

Too many of us are operating in 'safe mode'. We follow rules and norms that keep us playing smaller than we could. Do you ever hear yourself saying (or even thinking!) things like this?

- "I can't say that. I might upset her."
- "I've got to do it this way because that's what everyone else does."
- "It's too dangerous to try that. Things might get out of control."
- "Well, that's just the way things are."

We all do it. As a result, we're limiting our choices, and our effectiveness.

Yes, sometimes there's a need for 'safe mode'. And the more robust your system, the less you'll need to use it.

In 2015, PwC published an insightful report called *The Hidden Talent*, which pointed to the idea that the challenges we face today require a different type of leader. One who's not merely good at achieving results, but is also extraordinarily adept at creating and leading business change in complex environments. The report shows that while 52% of leaders are great at getting stuff done, only 8% of leaders are effective 'strategists', meaning they are highly effective at generating organisational and personal transformation.

In this great unfreezing, as the ice rapidly melts, we can choose to be blindly carried along by the wave created by these forces of change, or we can learn how to harness them to our (and others') advantage. The better we are at being in uncertainty, the more we will be able to take advantage of it. Otherwise we are swimming around in the melted white water at its mercy.

Interesting times arise when there's a gap between what we're used to, and have got comfortable with, and what the world is asking of us now. You could say it's kind of like being in the middle of two elastic bands, being pulled in opposite directions. One end is screaming "Stay put!", and the other is yelling "We need you to be over here!" That's an uncomfortable tension. It's like teetering on a threshold. You can handle it for a while, but it's debilitating. Eventually, something's got to give. You have to move one way or the other.

To make sense of and seize the opportunities in front of us, we need to cultivate a Change Maker mindset and action orientation. We need to cross a threshold from one way of being to another.

AT THE THRESHOLD

All great acts of genius began with the same consideration: Do not be constrained by your present reality.

LEONARDO DA VINCI

THE WAY THINGS ARE

When I was about six years old, my grandparents went on a cruise ship from Perth to Bali, Indonesia. That was back in the day when you were allowed to go on board the ship and visit when it was in port, which is what my family planned to do. Except I was terrified of going on board. I had a story in my head that the ship would sink in port, and everyone would drown. I have no idea where I got that story from, but I absolutely believed it to be true, and there was no way I was going on board that boat. So, I waited on shore with my poor Mum, while my Dad and brother went aboard for an adventure. Clearly they didn't have the same story in their heads about cruise ships that I did.

Have you ever looked back at a time in your life where you now say "I can't believe I thought like that!" with a little embarrassment and laughter? You've since upgraded your story about how the world works to a more sophisticated one.

We all have stories about 'the way things are'. The way that *X* will happen if I do *Y*. The way things get done around here. What it's like in that foreign country. What's OK and what's not OK to do around a certain person. That a ship will sink while in port if I step on board.

Stories about 'the way things are' can be useful. They help us short-circuit our thinking process. They provide metaphorical channels for the water of our minds to be directed down. With stories about the way things are, it can make our decision-making process easier. Robert Cialdini, in his book *Influence*, describes them as 'psychological shortcuts'. Here's what he says:

> *We simply must [use psychological shortcuts], because the world is a complex place where it's impossible for us to ponder the details of every decision we make. Thus, we use quick shortcuts, and most of the time they serve us well.*

Stories about 'the way things are' are shortcuts. They're frames to help us make sense of the world. And frames, by their very nature, have limitations. Sometimes the frames that we put around stories are too small to represent the real picture within it. Sometimes the story is just plain wrong.

Interesting times bring us to a threshold where we have to make some choices. When we arrive at the threshold, we bring assumptions about the way things are, and they can limit us from taking the next step. If we are to continue our journey, it's useful to stop, examine the assumptions, and perhaps change them.

Here are some of the assumptions we can bring to the threshold that can stop us from choosing to cross it wholeheartedly. Let's stress-test these assumptions, and look at a few alternatives.

Before the threshold, we chase:	Beyond the threshold, we embrace:
• Certainty	• Curiosity
• Conformity	• Authenticity
• Stability	• Dynamism
What we end up with:	**What we end up getting:**
• Restless frustration	• Vibrant creativity

FROM CERTAINTY TO CURIOSITY

The quest for certainty blocks the search for meaning. Uncertainty is the very condition to impel man to unfold his powers.

ERICH FROMM

Certainty is overrated.

Yet our brains crave it. Certainty helps us make predictions more confidently, so we can operate in the world without having to use a huge amount of mental resources for each and every activity.

According to David Rock of the Neuroleadership Institute, when we don't know what happens next, our brains invest extra neural energy to try to create the certainty we crave. Using that energy can leave us debilitated and distracted from the present.

Our Western culture upholds a narrative that all things should be certain. When our leaders can't give us certainty amidst change, they're lambasted for appearing weak or dithering. When our doctor can't tell us for certain what it is that ails us, we seek a second opinion. When the weather forecasters get it wrong, we say they're hopeless.

Nothing is certain, and we're better off when we live with that in mind. Uncertainty can be a powerful catalyst to help us to feel more deeply alive. A relative degree of uncertainty can pique our curiosity and interest, and opens a window of opportunity to create what we want. Rather than saying, "I need to know what will happen next", we can say, "Right, I wonder what's over that horizon?"

It's like learning to ride a bike. If we waited until we knew we wouldn't fall off before we tried to learn it, we'd never try it. And we'd never learn what it takes. The need for certainty smothers the drive to learn.

The great explorers didn't need certainty when they left their familiar surroundings. They needed curiosity. The same goes for all of us. When we've chosen to face uncertainty and do something for ourselves rather than wait to be told the answer, we come through to the other side with a new level of insight. Even if we get tripped up in the process, we're likely to learn something.

In interesting times, the challenge is not to get rid of the need for certainty, but instead to learn to live with a paradox:

to create more certainty in your ability to deal with uncertainty.

....

NOTHING IS CERTAIN, AND WE'RE BETTER OFF WHEN WE LIVE WITH THAT IN MIND.

FROM CONFORMITY TO AUTHENTICITY

*Conformity is the jailer of freedom
and the enemy of growth.*

JOHN F. KENNEDY

Conformity has its place. Standards, norms, and rules keep things running smoothly. As a species, we humans have thrived on the planet because we've learned to coexist in groups that are bound by rules and customs.

In interesting times, rules and customs need to be tested. In a changing environment, what got us here won't necessarily get us there. Rather than uphold conformity for its own sake, the more useful approach is to look at the reason behind the rule, and explore its purpose and usefulness in the current context.

When I was around 13 years old, I read the classic *Jonathan Livingston Seagull* by Richard Bach. Yes, it's a book about seagulls. According to flock lore, the purpose of life is to stay alive, and the means to do that is to fly out to sea and catch fish. Jonathan is a seagull who thinks this is rubbish. He's way more interested in flying for the pure joy of flying. As a result, he's seen as a rebel, and is outcast from the flock. In his solo life, Jonathan turns his attention to mastering all aspects of flying, and in the process, he develops an inner sense of power and confidence. He also develops a deep compassion for the flock, seeing how stuck and limited they are in their conformity. Upon his return, he begins to help others in the flock see what's possible beyond conformity. A Change Maker in action, right there.

Jonathan's story is an example of what mythologist Joseph Campbell calls the Hero's Journey – the transcendence from conformity and a mundane existence into self-discovery and growth. The Hero's Journey is a journey of struggle, danger, adventure, and challenge, and it's a story that each one of us needs to live if we are to find our voice and make the difference we want to make.

Conformity can keep us safe, but clinging to the norm because the alternative is too risky is even more dangerous. We'll never truly discover what we're capable of.

Change Making requires you to step up, take the Hero's Journey, and go for what you truly believe in. Even when it's against the grain of what everyone else thinks. When we embrace authenticity over conformity, we are on our way.

FROM STABILITY TO DYNAMISM

Stability leads to instability. The more stable things become, and the longer things are stable, the more unstable they will be when the crisis hits.

HYMAN MINSKY

Stability is temporary.

When people talk about achieving 'work–life balance' and other such notions, I get the impression that they've got some nirvana in mind where everything is perfectly sorted. There are no tensions or conflicts to solve. Nothing changes. Everything's stable.

Sounds boring to me.

Beyond boring, it's not actually how life works.

Hyman Minsky was a maverick economist who observed that as financial markets chase stability, they actually become more unstable, and less resilient to shocks. His ideas were considered novel at the time, but not really taken seriously. Until the global financial crisis hit, that is. Now Minsky's ideas have regained interest in mainstream financial markets.

If we make stability the goal, we're always going to be working against the laws of nature. We're at risk of trying to build a house of cards in a wind tunnel.

I reckon life works better for us if we accept the idea of dynamism, where everything is in constant motion *and* perfectly balanced.

Let's explore that idea. Imagine someone on a seesaw:

'Nirvana' is when the seesaw is perfectly flat. Maybe that might happen when no one's on it. But when there's a person on it, there's always going to be some movement. It's always going to tip one way or the other. Even if it's just a little bit:

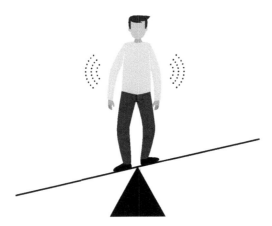

It's kind of like when you ride a bike: you're always countering the way the bike wants to naturally fall. That's just what you do.

If you accept that this is how life works, then your work is not really about achieving a static 'balanced' state. That's futile. Your work is about learning to move with the forces. It's about noticing when it tips too far one way, and adapting to bring it back the other way. Then noticing again. And adapting again. And so on. Until it becomes unconscious and that's just what you do, without breaking a sweat.

There is always going to be some form of 'tipping'. Conflicting choices, competing tensions.

The more adept we are at dancing with the forces at play, the better we are able to embrace the realities of life, and therefore have a chance at changing them.

There is no such thing as static balance. There never will be.

CHANGE MAKERS ARE ALWAYS EVOLVING.

To evolve, it's a good idea to examine some of the stories you're telling yourself. Those stories were good for getting you to where you are today, but, as uber-coach Marshall Goldsmith says, "What got you here won't get you there."

....

CHANGE MAKING REQUIRES YOU
TO STEP UP, TAKE THE HERO'S
JOURNEY, AND GO FOR WHAT
YOU TRULY BELIEVE IN.

THRIVING VS SURVIVING

When you cross the threshold, when you begin to transcend the driving need to chase certainty, conformity, stability, and the like, interesting things happen:

- **You realise you don't need permission.**
  Beyond the threshold, you realise that the only person that needs to give you permission is yourself.

- **You realise that rules can be up for negotiation.**
  Beyond the threshold, rules are still important, but you challenge the 'why' behind the rule. You see that if stuff can get done in a faster or better way while minimising the downsides, then it's worthwhile challenging it.

- **You realise that playing it safe isn't worth it.**
  Beyond the threshold, you realise that playing it safe is a waste of time. You've tasted the vibrant fruits of boldness, and when you let go of safety, the world opens up.

If you want to make an impact, cross the threshold. You've done it before. You can do it again!

Beyond the threshold, here's what you experience:

- You see and feel the impact of your ideas actually making a difference, because you've had the courage and savvy to put them out there.

- You can withstand the knocks better, because you're grounded in a deep sense of conviction. In fact, you welcome them because of the learning they can give you.

- You attract other Change Makers and start to build a coalition. Like attracts like.

- You see your team, office, organisation, industry, and maybe even your country become more agile, vibrant, and thriving as a result of your efforts.

- You leave behind the restless frustration and embrace vibrant creativity. You just feel more alive.

You've probably experienced some these before, right? Let's get you getting more of them.

The people who thrive in interesting times are the ones who master the skills to create the outcomes they want. They listen to and act on the voice that calls them 'over here'. They lean into the discomfort that interesting times bring, rather than avoid it. They are the Change Makers and they make the future. And you are one of them.

While there have always been interesting times, the one you are living in right now is the one you need to deal with. So, if you're going to navigate these times successfully, it's worth mapping out what it will take to do so.

THE PEOPLE WHO THRIVE IN
INTERESTING TIMES ARE THE
ONES WHO MASTER THE SKILLS
TO CREATE THE OUTCOMES
THEY WANT.

Crossing the Threshold: Carl Sanders-Edwards

Carl is the CEO and Founder of Adeption, a company dedicated to changing leadership behaviour through combining artificial intelligence, design thinking, and behavioural science into a clever app. Carl's overriding focus for the past 18 years is on helping people and workplaces perform better.

Here's Carl in his own words about crossing the threshold:

I grew up in a small New Zealand town called Thames. It was my world, and life was good. I loved the outdoors and was into all sorts of local activities.

And, I had the opportunity to go to university. The bulk of people from school didn't head off to university, so back then it felt like a big decision. Making it even harder was a chance to go work in the outdoors at a stunning camping resort at the top of the Coromandel, driving boats, guiding tourists, an 18-year-old's dream! And while I loved this idea, I really wanted to study, and open a new page. So it was a big decision about whether I should or not. It's crazy thinking back about it now, but it felt like that was a big move to move away from home. To move away from the comfort zone and everyone that I knew. Going to university was a divergent path. Something in me just said, "No, I'm going to go live and learn and do this thing."

And that created a massive shift. Academically I performed way better than I ever had at school. When I got away from all the expectations of my growing up, I became more of my own person. I found a whole lot of parts about myself that I never really knew I had. And the interesting thing is, none of that other stuff went away. So, all the stuff that I thought I was giving up, like being in the outdoors, didn't go away. I just added to it. The university was near the beach, so I picked up surfing. I wasn't interested in surfing before then. As a result, going back to visit home was even better!

Making that decision to leave home was a formative experience for me, and the lessons I took from that have played out in my life ever since.

More recently, I'd been building a business and had built a strong reputation here locally. We had a massive contract with one of New Zealand's largest companies. At the same time, I got a scholarship to go and study MBA at Babson in the US, which I accepted. You wouldn't believe the number of people who said, "You're crazy. You're going to go and study to learn how to do what you've just done. And if you go, you're going to go and ruin it." And it's pretty much what happened in the first six months I was over there. The whole thing imploded. All of those prophesies were coming true. However, in the long run we got there, and the results are better for the experience.

In hindsight, what it did was just like what happened when I went to university. It just opened up another whole side of myself. Before that, I'd developed a strong process-focus and was very disciplined in my work, and that had given me a really good foundation. Doing the MBA, I discovered that I was way more naturally creative. I was way more messy in my thinking. I was way more entrepreneurial, and now people meet me, and they have no idea how I could have ever studied engineering. Doing that gave me permission to access that whole side of myself. As a result, I just created another big breakthrough. And it takes time, obviously, but it was a big phase.

Now we're doing it again. We're launching the business in the US. It's crazy risky. We've built a good strong business in New Zealand that's continuing to grow. And it's actually the perfect time to go and shake it up a bit.

CHAPTER TWO: THE CHANGE MAKER'S JOURNEY

RESTLESS

In the original *Star Wars* movie, there's a scene early on when we meet our hero, Luke Skywalker. He's stuck on Tatooine, his home planet, where nothing much happens. Restless and frustrated, he's looking for something more than life working on the farm with his uncle and aunt. His head is full of stories from other star systems, and of heroes doing great deeds. But he feels grounded by the expectations and needs of his family. He's looking for a way out, but can't find it. He's stuck.

Many compelling stories begin with this type of scenario – the protagonist living a day-to-day existence, dreaming of something different, but not having the wherewithal to make it happen. One of the reasons we're drawn to such stories is that we can see ourselves in them.

Most of us can relate to Luke's dilemma as part of our own experience. Feeling stuck, torn between a possible future and the expectations of a current reality. That restlessness and wheel spinning, feeling like time is ticking by and you're wasting away while it's all happening around you.

If you're familiar with the story, you'll know that Luke does find a way out of Tatooine. He goes on to discover who he is and how he can make a difference.

Let's begin to look how we can make that happen for you.

SEEKING

Of the thousands of people that I've coached and had as participants in my leadership workshops and programmes, I'd estimate the distribution looks something like this:

- Roughly one quarter have a predominantly 'maker' mindset, actively going for it to make positive change happen in their worlds. They might be terrified, they might not have all the tools they need, but they're restless and they're on a mission.

- The rest have a predominantly 'waiter' mindset. Some are waiting for inspiration. Others are waiting for someone else to give them permission to make change happen. And some others are waiting for someone or something else to do most of the changing. Some might be waiting for all of this change to go away.

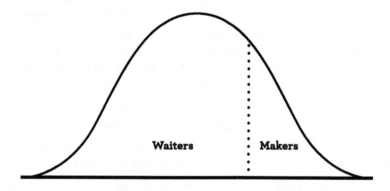

My experience reflects research in the adult development field by former Harvard developmental psychologist Robert Kegan, which shows:

- Approximately 25% of adults operate from a 'self-authored' mindset. Their thinking and behaviours are primarily guided by a strong inner sense of vision, values, and purpose that trumps any fear they might experience. They have an experimental, curious nature and are willing to take action in the face of uncertainty. These people are far more effective at creating and leading positive change.

- The bulk of the rest operate from a 'socialised' mindset. These people take their cues about 'what's right' to do from external authority sources (e.g. senior leaders, parents, social norms). The fear of bad things happening by trying something new overwhelms any positive action. The research suggests that people with a socialised mind have a more limited impact in making and sustaining positive change. (For more on Robert Kegan's research and thinking, check out his RSA talk at https://bit.ly/2S6h6QG)

Which category might you fall into?

In my experience, within the 'waiter' group, there's a large category of restless people who are on the cusp, close to the top of the curve. They want to make a difference, but they're frustrated and ineffective. They're the restless go-getters who are spinning their wheels, trying to get traction. They're seeking something but haven't yet 'locked on'.

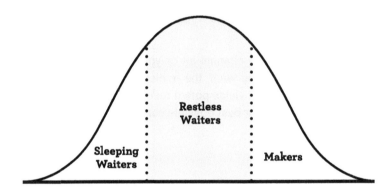

Maybe you've experienced some of these:

- You can see what needs to happen, but you can't for the life of you see how you're going to make it happen.
- You feel like a lone voice and no one's listening.
- You're passionate, but you may be playing a little safer than you need to.
- You're banging your head against a brick wall, putting in the effort but getting nowhere.
- You have ideas that just won't go away!

WE NEED YOUR IMPACT

This restless feeling is totally normal. Being restless is a critical part of becoming a successful Change Maker, and one that you'll always want to keep with you. Restlessness is the fuel of change.

But it's not enough.

The discontent that we experience with restlessness usually stems from a combination of two factors:

- **An inner drive to make a difference**
  You've woken up to what's possible and are seeking what mythologist Joseph Campbell calls a real 'experience of being alive'.

- **A lack of clear perspective and focus**
  You're energised to move, but lack direction. Each individual effort is well intentioned but together they lack a coherent strategy to be effective.

Combined, these factors are a recipe for burnout, frustration, and disillusionment.

When you have a way to channel all of your thinking and behaviours towards creating what you want, the restlessness subsides and gives way to focused effort that yields potent results. If you don't harness the restlessness, we miss your best possible contributions. And our world is the poorer for it.

RESTLESSNESS IS THE
FUEL OF CHANGE.

FROM SLEEPER TO MAKER

Nothing starts as a finished product. Including you, right? Becoming an effective Change Maker is an ongoing process of development. None of us are perfect. But we can learn as we go.

The journey to becoming a successful Change Maker is like learning to navigate a maze. The more perspective you have, the easier it gets. It's often messy and confusing, and sometimes we don't even know where to begin!

Here's a map that outlines a Change Maker's developmental journey:

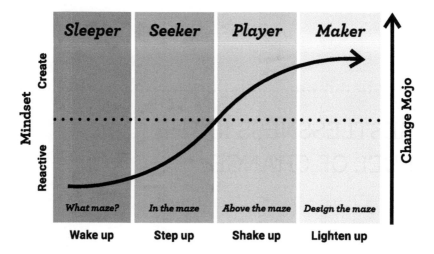

There are four stages, each one higher than the last. To shift from one stage to the next, you cross a threshold where you let go of some old habits and mindsets and adopt some new ones.

As you go, you grow your Change Mojo. The word 'mojo' comes from Africa, where it means magic charm or spell. Your Change Mojo is your magic power to make change happen. The more of it you have, the more effective you can be.

Let's look at each of the stages and their thresholds in sequence.

SLEEPER – *WHAT MAZE?*

A mind stretched by a new idea can never return to its old dimensions.

OLIVER WENDELL HOLMES

A Sleeper is the most passive level of Change Maker. Like someone who's actually asleep, someone with a Sleeper's perspective is somewhat ignorant to the environment around them. They might be in denial, or just plain naive. Or perhaps they just haven't lived enough yet.

Sleepers don't make change, change happens to them. It's a bit like being Neo in the movie *The Matrix*. At first, he doesn't even realise he's in a constructed world. *The Matrix* is a story about waking up and seeing reality for what it is.

While ignorance is bliss, in our fast-changing world, reality has a nasty habit of sneaking up and sideswiping you in the head when you least expect it. Having a Sleeper perspective limits you to solely being subject to the forces of change, rather than being an active agent of change. Like the story of the frog being slowly boiled to death in a pot of water that's heating up, we can be ignorant until it's too late. The work at Sleeper is to *wake up*.

Given you're reading this book, it's highly unlikely you're in Sleeper mode. That said, we are all 'asleep' to some degree. There are always things we're unaware of, things that we don't know. Those 'unknown unknowns'. By cultivating your own awareness that you don't know everything, you avoid falling into Sleeper mode.

SEEKER – *IN THE MAZE*

When we tire of well-worn ways, we seek for new. This restless craving in the souls of men spurs them to climb, and to seek the mountain view.

ELLA WHEELER WILCOX

When you're at the Seeker stage, you've joined a tribe of people who have chosen to play a game that's beyond the norm. Author James Kavanaugh, in his book *There Are Men Too Gentle To Live Among Wolves*, calls them 'searchers':

> *Some people do not have to search. They find their niche early in life and rest there, seemingly contented and resigned. They do not seem to ask much of life, sometimes they do not seem to take it seriously. At times I envy them, but usually I do not understand them. Seldom do they understand me.*

> *I am one of the searchers. There are, I believe, millions of us. We are not unhappy, but neither are we really content. We continue to explore life, hoping to uncover its ultimate secret. We continue to explore ourselves, hoping to understand.*

Seekers are by definition restless. At Seeker, you're 'awake' and keen to make change happen. However, you're probably not getting as much traction as you'd like. You're seeking a direction, seeking an answer. Seeking a way forward. Perhaps seeking something that will bring you more alive. You're wandering through the maze and going around in circles.

Here are some things people commonly seek:

- Permission
- Direction
- Certainty
- Clarity
- Perfection
- Power
- The answer
- The right time

Which ones apply to you?

The focus at Seeker is to *step up*. That's about giving your inner drive the focus it needs. Stepping up means deciding what your priorities are and what game you want to be in. It's about refining and tapping into your sense of purpose. It's about becoming more self-authored and beginning to deliberately write your next chapter. It's about deciding what you won't tolerate anymore. It's about finding the courage to live more on your own terms, and less on what others, and society at large, tells you those terms should be.

Many leaders and Change Makers that I've worked with know the Seeker experience well. It's a natural place to be, and in fact is a critical part of the journey. Without first seeking, we're not going to go anywhere! And we won't develop the solid foundations to make lasting change happen.

Seeker is more than a stage to move through. The skills you develop at Seeker are skills you will continue to rely on throughout your Change Making journey. We should never stop seeking.

FROM REACTIVE TO CREATIVE

Everyone thinks of changing the world, but no one thinks of changing himself.

LEO TOLSTOY

Change Makers have an orientation to the world that is fundamentally different to others.

Quite simply, they focus on creating more of what they want to see in the world, rather than simply reacting to what the world asks of them.

As you move along the Change Maker curve, there's a fundamental shift that you make at the point where you transition from Seeker to Player. That's the shift from a below-the-line 'Reactive' orientation to the world to an above-the-line 'Creative' orientation.

Reactive

When we believe external circumstances are the driving force in our life, and obstacles are problems to be solved, it's difficult for us to make lasting change happen. This is what Robert Fritz, author of *The Path of Least Resistance*, calls the Reactive Mind.

When our default mode is to react to external forces, success will be limited and fleeting. We get caught in a cycle of trying to make problems go away so we can 'get back to normal', only to have them pop up again later. We've all been here, and it's frustrating, right? A common example is the need to please others. If we're driven by others' approval, we'll use great strategies to avoid conflict and keep the other person happy. But that's not creating change, that's just trying to keep things at a level. We stay safe, but we don't make any bow waves.

At Seeker, we can sometimes be focused on trying to change 'the other'. The other can be the organisation, the team, the boss. It's something outside of us. "I just wish they would change!" When we focus solely on changing 'the other', we're on a hiding to nothing. As Susan Scott, author of *Fierce Conversations*, says:

We're each responsible for 50% of every relationship we are in. If you want to change the relationship, change the 50% you have most control over: you!

Creative

On the other hand, if you believe you are the driving force in your life, and it's you that first must change if you are to change the world, you're operating out of what Robert Fritz calls the Creative Mind. With this mindset, obstacles aren't problems but opportunities, and you focus on actively creating what you most want. It's like a glider being untethered from the tow plane. The power now comes from you tapping into an unseen force, which in this case is your sense of purpose, vision, and efficacy. You're not tethered to an external authority anymore, and you can go where you want. At this point, there's less of a focus on solving problems to make them go away, and more of a focus on deciding what you want and making that happen. It's incredibly powerful and liberating to operate out of a Creative mindset.

Change Makers are well and truly proponents of the Creative mindset. As you read more about the Player and Maker stages below, bear this in mind.

PLAYER – *ABOVE THE MAZE*

The electric light did not come from the continuous improvement of candles.

OREN HARARI

Being a Player is to be in the game. When you're in the game, you're moving with purpose. You're now actively focused on building your effectiveness and making the impact you want to make. When you're a Player, you adopt a Creative mindset in everything you do. Things start to shift. You're getting solid momentum.

The main focus at Player is to *shake things up*. This means that while you're creating more of what you want to see in the world, you're OK with ruffling a few feathers as you do it. Including your own. As the saying goes, you can't make an omelette without breaking a few eggs. In an interview with Barack Obama, the host David Letterman says, "Nothing right in the world ever comes without a fight." Obama responds, "Or at least some discomfort." Being a Player comes with a few risks.

The work at the Player stage is about getting comfortable with being uncomfortable. With things getting messy and staying that way for a while. Shaking it up requires resilience and persistence over time.

MAKER – *DESIGN THE MAZE*

A trained mind is better than any script.

EPICTETUS

With a Player perspective, you're active, busy, and super-focused. With a Maker perspective, you're probably still active and busy, but you're walking just that bit more lightly.

It's a bit like being an accomplished musician in a cool jazz band. You know the few fundamental structural elements that define the tune you're playing, and within those boundaries you can take it wherever you want. Sometimes, you take the lead. Other times, others take the lead. You're playing stuff you've probably never played before, and you've got the confidence and skill to explore what's possible. Your focus is less on nailing it, and more about shaping it. You acutely sense where the music is going, and you play your part to contribute to that.

As a Maker, you get out of your own way, see the broader system at play, and invent new pathways. Makers don't just see the maze, they design the maze.

The focus at Maker is to *lighten up*. At this point, you know the rules and you've got the tools. You can now start to have more fun with things, to experiment and play with boundaries, and barbeque a few sacred cows. You take yourself less seriously, while still taking the work seriously.

Here's how to spot a Maker. They:
- Appear to have a great depth of wisdom and perspective on the world.
- Have a paradoxical blend of deep gravitas and refreshing lightness about them.
- Are pretty much ego-free. They don't take themselves too seriously, and they're deeply humble.
- Use humour to create human connection.
- Have an elegant economy of effort. They put in just the right amount of effort at just the right time.

Jim Collins conducted a landmark study of organisations to understand what takes a company from merely good to truly great. As reported in his book *Good to Great*, all of the great companies were led through the transition by what he calls 'Level Five' leaders. These leaders possessed two critical qualities that set them apart: deep humility and fierce resolve. These are the marks of a true Change Maker.

In summary, here is the work to shift from Sleeper to Maker:

Stage	Task	Dial Down	Dial Up
Sleeper	Wake Up	Ignorance	Awareness
Seeker	Step Up	Frustration	Conviction
Player	Shake Up	Acceptance	Challenge
Maker	Lighten Up	Earnestness	Playfulness

MAKE YOUR MARK

The journey from Sleeper to Maker doesn't happen overnight. It's an ongoing process of development that asks you to look deeply at yourself and engage consciously with the world on a daily basis.

As you do this work, you can expect to see some shifts happening:

1. You're more focused.

The more you lock onto the type of change you want to see happen in the world, the more other things fade into the background. It doesn't mean you're not aware of them. They just have less importance now.

2. You have greater perspective.

While you're more focused, you can also see and appreciate more of the maze you're in. And as a result, you have a greater sense of choice about where to go and what to do next.

3. You have a bigger amplifying effect.

Something cool happens when you step up and begin to shake things up. Those ripples become bow waves. You're making your presence felt. And, yes, the water can get a little turbulent.

4. The turbulence becomes fun.

Because you're developing a greater sense of agency, you're less worried about how you might deal with what comes up next. You're building the confidence and ability to handle turbulence.

5. You're more 'you'.

Your contribution feels more authentically 'you'. There's less 'trying to be' and more just 'being'.

6. You make your mark, faster.

When you combine the other five factors above, progress is inevitable.

Priscila Bernades

"Making a difference in the world has always been a passion of mine."

Priscila Bernades is Head of Sales & Marketing for Lancom Technology, an IT support and software development company based in Auckland, New Zealand. She's also the HubSpot Ambassador for New Zealand, and is super-active in championing thought-leadership in her sector. She is well regarded as a role model for other women in a typically male-dominated profession.

Priscila comes from humble beginnings in Brazil, where her early life experiences shaped her profoundly.

> I remember thinking: I don't want to be an adult and be in this position. I want to fight for a better life. And I want to help other people to not have that same life. So how am I going to do that? By being a role model and trying myself.

Priscila started her first full-time job at the age of 14, becoming financially independent at the age of 17 (which included paying for her bachelor's degree). And she was continually restless.

> Even as a very young child, I was never settled for what I had. I always wanted to learn more, I was always very curious about things. I never settled for normal.

When she was 20, Priscila decided that she needed a new challenge, so she decided to come to New Zealand. At the time, she couldn't speak English.

> But I realised that I would learn, and there was no better place to learn than being in a position where you just have to speak it. It was hard at the beginning, not being able to communicate. I like to talk! Then I figured I just needed to start talking, to give it a go.

After being in the country for a week, she landed her first job as a dishwasher.

I was here for one week and one of the few things I learned how to say was, "I'm looking for a job and do you have a position available?"

Others were also going for the job, but she got it because of her conviction and courage.

The manager who employed me said to me, "I really liked your courage because I knew you couldn't understand me, but you sat down, and I knew you really wanted it, whereas I looked at the other girls and I didn't see that fire in their eyes."

From there, Priscila moved on to be a cleaner, and then to work in a restaurant. Within a few months, she decided that her goal was to be in a professional job within 12 months.

Through my cleaning work, I managed to create relationships with every single person that I was cleaning the houses for. And it's simple things. It's coming in, it's saying good morning, it's asking how they were, it's paying attention to the details. And I remember one day having a 30-second conversation with one of the people I was cleaning for and asking him what he did for work. And he told me, "I work with computers. If you ever need to buy a laptop, give me a call." And he gave me his card.

So, a few months later, I emailed him and said, "I'm Priscila, I'm the cleaner girl. I'm no longer cleaning. I'm looking to start a career in New Zealand. I thought I'd call you in case you know anyone that's possibly looking for someone." I didn't hear anything until a couple of weeks later. I got a reply saying, "Oh hey, Priscila, of course I remember you. How about we meet for a coffee on Tuesday, 3 o'clock?" It turned out that coffee was an interview, and I got hired on the spot.

Since then, Priscila has gone from strength to strength in her professional career, and has earned an MBA from the University of Auckland Business School.

Priscilla reflects on her journey:

I hear people talking about the stuff I have been through, and it's always a surprise in a way because I say, "Isn't that normal? Isn't that what people go through in life?" And then people say, "No, no that's quite special. That's quite interesting, you've got a story to tell here." So, my intention to be a role model is almost happening just by me following my own path and going for it.

And the result of that is, you know, no matter what happens, the way I look at things these days, almost nothing scares me because I've tested myself in so many new situations already. I've tested and grown my ability to deal with the unknown.

CHANGE MAKERS HAVE AN ORIENTATION TO THE WORLD THAT IS FUNDAMENTALLY DIFFERENT TO OTHERS.

Part Two:

BEING A CHANGE MAKER

CHAPTER THREE: THE FOUR C'S OF CHANGE MAKING

HEAT SEEKERS

A couple of years ago, one of my clients, a large public sector organisation, asked me to meet with a range of their leaders to debrief their 360-degree feedback. The organisation was going through a sustained period of huge turbulence and change. Sound familiar? I met over 30 leaders during a couple of weeks. As that time unfolded, I noticed an interesting theme emerging. The leaders who were rated the most effective, in this changing environment, by far, had similar patterns in their own backgrounds and stories. More specifically:

- They'd cultivated a deep sense of purpose or conviction that grounded them.
- They held a deep curiosity about the world and their place in it.
- They'd deliberately fostered mutually beneficial relationships with a wide range of people, including people who challenge them.
- They'd sought out a significant degree of change and stretch in their own careers.

Let's break these points down a little more.

I observed a certain 'groundedness' about them. Not detachment; on the contrary, they were purposeful and passionate about making a difference. It was more that they were like the person who steers the white-water raft: there's craziness all around them, but they've been in similar situations before and have a deep confidence in their ability to navigate the volatility. They were grounded.

They were intensely curious. These people were voracious learners. They had a deep interest in a wide range of subjects, not simply their areas of expertise. They were quick to ask questions and slow to judge. Most dedicated time to reflect and make sense of things. I also noticed they were the keenest to take on board and make sense of their feedback, as if they saw it as another way to learn about themselves and how they were perceived in the eyes of others. And as a result, I got the sense they had a clear and real sense of who they were and what they stood for.

They sought out and created valuable relationships. They deliberately cultivated their networks, which included mentors, coaches, people with different perspectives to their own, people whom they could help, and those who could help them. Most strikingly, they all valued having people around them that challenged them. One summed it up nicely: "I need people who keep me on my learning edge." They didn't necessarily want 'comfy' relationships, but interesting ones instead.

Their career paths weren't linear. Their backgrounds included multiple roles in different industries, often in different countries. While their career paths told a story of ongoing evolution, as most résumés do, there was something deeper at play. Their changes weren't forced upon them – they created them themselves. There was something in their stories about the courage to break away from the norm and pursue some sort of calling, even though they knew it'd be difficult and scary. Taking the 'road not taken', as Robert Frost would say.

These people were the ones rated most highly as leaders. Were these the only qualities that made them stand out? No, they were also all technically proficient and reasonably smart. They all had strong emotional intelligence. These are the 'price of entry' qualities that get you into the game of effective leadership and change-making in turbulent times. But they alone don't guarantee you'll thrive.

There are a few key qualities that make the difference to whether we thrive or just merely survive during interesting times. Beyond the technical skills required for specific roles, there are four meta-skills that are fast becoming prized regardless of role or industry. These are *Conviction, Curiosity, Connection, and Courage.*

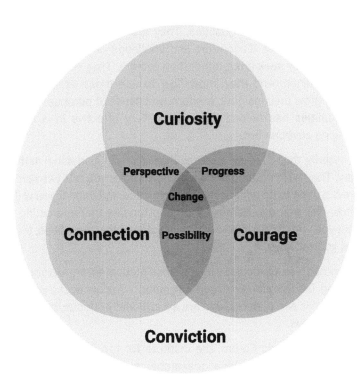

Your **conviction** is your fuel.

Your **curiosity** keeps you learning.

Your **connection** is your bridge to others.

Your **courage** is what creates change.

These people had these qualities. They are what I call 'heat-seekers'. They've learned that discomfort and challenge is good for their own growth, and they seek it out rather than avoid it. They seek to learn from every experience. And they know how to use those experiences, and people, to grow their insights, wisdom, and sense of purpose. Cultivating these qualities has helped them to be very effective in a changing, challenging environment.

More broadly, these are the qualities that underpin leadership in the 21st century. They have nothing to do with how senior you are. However, they have everything to do with how much influence and impact you will have, and how well you can harness the opportunities that interesting times present you with. The more you have developed these qualities, the more impact you will have.

Savvy companies, particularly in disrupted industries, are looking for, and appointing, leaders who embrace disruption, can connect across diverse demographics and cultures, and are exceptionally curious, open-minded, and courageous.

The World Economic Forum, the Institute for the Future, and futurists such as Bob Johansen have all researched and reported on the types of work skills required for 2020 and beyond. In synthesising their findings, the conclusion is that we need to shift from a world that values Certainty, Conformity, and Stability to one that embraces Conviction, Curiosity, Connection, and Courage.

CONVICTION

Conviction is what you have when you've cultivated a deep sense of purpose, a reason for being, a sense of what you most want to have happen in the world. It's about being connected to a deep driving force to make a difference to something beyond yourself. In the diagram, it circles the other three C's because it's like the glue that makes the whole thing work.

CURIOSITY

Curiosity is the insatiable drive to:

- Ask questions, learn, unlearn, and sit with ambiguity and 'not knowing'.
- Step back, critique, and make sense of things objectively.
- Seek and find deeper meaning in the patterns.
- See things from new and different perspectives.
- Have novel and adaptive thinking.

CONNECTION

Connection is the desire and ability to:

- Seek out and connect meaningfully with a diverse range of people.
- Apply social intelligence.
- Serve others.
- Collaborate effectively in a wide array of settings.

In particular, the ability to deliberately cultivate an effective network is an essential skill in interesting times.

COURAGE

To have courage is to:

- Act without being assured of success.
- Act without needing approval or permission.
- Experiment, innovate, and try new approaches.
- Be agile.
- Challenge existing ideas and practices, including your own.

As human beings, we all have the seeds of these in us. Some are more developed than others.

Ask yourself: What would be the value to me in developing more of each of these?

WORK THE INTERSECTIONS

When you deliberately cultivate and combine these qualities in your own authentic way, you generate fresh *perspectives*, create new *possibilities*, and get accelerated *progress* on your change initiatives.

CURIOSITY + CONNECTION = PERSPECTIVE

When you're intensely curious, and you can connect with other people, you have a great chance of seeing your challenge with a fresh perspective. When you're open to having your own assumptions and beliefs shaken up and tested a little, you can see things with new eyes. The ability to look at things from multiple perspectives, rather than just your own, is a significant skill in a fast-changing world where relying solely on your own experience and assumptions can mean you miss the point entirely.

CONNECTION + COURAGE = POSSIBILITY

When you connect with people courageously, you generate new possibilities. This is the realm of speaking your truth, telling powerful stories, and having courageous conversations. It's about being vulnerable in front of others. It's about stepping out from behind yourself and being real. As Marianne Williamson said:

> As we let our own light shine, we unconsciously give other people permission to do the same. As we are liberated from our own fear, our presence automatically liberates others.

When we step out from behind ourselves and connect with others in a real, authentic way, we generate possibilities not before seen.

CURIOSITY + COURAGE = PROGRESS

Curiosity is the fuel that ignites your new ideas and keeps you learning. Curious people are generally great idea generators. But ideas are nothing without action. If you want to make an impact, you need to take that idea and test it. Of course, trying something new usually requires some courage. Curiosity has a price, and it's often the one that's paid when your actions bump up against the status quo. Curiosity in action is liable to bring you into conflict with authority. This is where courage comes in. As George Bernard Shaw said, "Progress is impossible without change." For change to happen, we need new ideas plus new action, which usually requires a good dose of courage.

WHEN WE STEP OUT FROM
BEHIND OURSELVES AND
CONNECT WITH OTHERS IN A
REAL, AUTHENTIC WAY, WE
GENERATE POSSIBILITIES
NOT BEFORE SEEN.

CHANGE MAKERS
SELF-ASSESSMENT

Complete this self-assessment.
Then, based on your answers, go
to the chapters that pique your
interest the most.

1 = Nowhere near it	**3** = Doing well
2 = Getting there	**4** = Got this nailed

Conviction

I have a clear, compelling sense of purpose in my work.	1	2	3	4
I'm clear about the type of impact I want to make in the world.	1	2	3	4
I know what it means to be at my best, and I aim to be that version of myself every day.	1	2	3	4

Curiosity

I'm an insatiable learner in everything I do.	1	2	3	4
When faced with unfamiliar situations I keep an open mind rather than rush to conclusions.	1	2	3	4
I regularly take time to reflect (e.g. I do regular journaling).	1	2	3	4

Connection

I've cultivated, and consistently leverage, a deep and diverse network of relationships to help me make change happen.	1	2	3	4
I have empathy – I can connect with people quickly and deeply.	1	2	3	4
I'm great at connecting people with ideas in ways that influence and impact.	1	2	3	4

Courage

I deliberately do one thing each day that stretches me.	1	2	3	4
I'm comfortable being known as someone who challenges the status quo.	1	2	3	4
I seek the tough feedback that I need to hear.	1	2	3	4

CHAPTER FOUR: CONVICTION

What is it you plan to do with your one wild, precious life?

MARY OLIVER

Christine Langdon is a social entrepreneur with a passion for helping people to experience the joy of giving. She is the co-founder and Chief of Good at The Good Registry (thegoodregistry.com), a social enterprise that simplifies giving, helps good causes, and reduces waste.

Have you ever said 'no gifts please' but still received gifts you don't need? Do gifts from the past clutter your cupboards, drawers, and shelves? Have you ever wondered what was spent on those gifts, and how much good it could do for needy causes instead? The Good Registry exists to help answer those questions.

Before becoming CE and Chief of Good, Christine was Community Manager at Z Energy, where she led the development and implementation of Z's Community Strategy – a multi-million dollar programme of charitable giving, skilled volunteering, and social wellbeing initiatives. It was a great job and a great place to work. She couldn't see any other job that she could possibly want. Yet...

Christine knew that she's a person who's always going somewhere with new challenges or adventures. "I can't just get comfortable where I am." She had that restless gene. She also knew that she didn't want another job, and she had a sense that she wanted to create a social enterprise of some sort. She just didn't know what. She decided that to get clarity on her next move, she needed to 'empty her glass'. In her own words:

> Life was full. Life was good, and I needed to take myself to ground zero and just create space to figure out what it was that I was going to create. So I left Z Energy to do nothing, and to create the space for something new, and because I knew that I couldn't do nothing, and I would need accountability, I decided to commit to living more

mindfully and to write a blog about that, and see what came up from doing that.

Four weeks later when I was noodling on what gives me joy, I came up with those four essentials of joy for me – kindness, connection, creativity, and presence. Then the idea for The Good Registry came after another week or two noodling on, "Okay, well how could I create an enterprise which gives others joy and me joy using those four pillars?"

I'm really clear that when your life is full, you're not going to have creative ideas or feel like you've got the space to try things or just see the ideas. It's the full glass analogy. You need to empty the glass out first.

Christine's decisions have been led by her values and a deep sense of conviction that her next move was in the social enterprise space, and it would be something she would create. Her awareness of the finite nature of her time on the planet was also a factor:

To me, one of the biggest drivers is knowing that time is short. We can stay comfortable, and the risk is that you stay comfortable for another five years and then you get knocked over by a bus. Then you don't get that opportunity that you were waiting for the right time to do. If something's worth doing, it's worth doing now.

CONVICTION IS YOUR FUEL

I think it's important to have a future that is inspiring and appealing. There has to be reasons you get up in the morning and want to live. Why do you want to live? What's the point? What inspires you? What do you love about the future?

ELON MUSK

Do you recall those times when you've felt a deep conviction? Like that time you so said 'no' to that enticing big party with all your mates because studying mattered more? Or that time when you found the courage to call someone out on their bad behaviour because, well, it just mattered too much not to?

Conviction is when you have a strongly held sense of belief about something that matters to you. When it's at its strongest, it springs from a deep sense of purpose. When you come across people with conviction, you'll hear them say things like:

- "This is what I'm here for."
- "I love this. I couldn't do anything else."
- "I'm focused. Nothing else matters right now."

The root of the word 'conviction' is also the root of the word 'convinced', as in "I'm utterly convinced". Conviction is what you have when you hold a deep belief about what's important, and you act on it. Conviction is that thing that keeps us moving when others fall by the wayside. Conviction helps us find the energy and courage to do what it takes when the stakes are high.

CONVICTION VS SECURITY

Change Makers define security differently to others. For Change Makers, security isn't something the world gives you. It's not 'out there' needing to be chased down.

For Change Makers, security lives 'in here'. When you've cultivated a deep sense of conviction for something that you truly want to make happen, a sense of security is part of the package. Your conviction provides you with the firm ground on which to stand.

As Helen Keller said:

> Security is mostly a superstition. It does not exist in nature, nor do the children of men as a whole experience it. Avoiding danger is no safer in the long run than outright exposure.

CONVICTION VS INTENTIONS

You can have lots of intentions, but do you have conviction?

Intentions are a head thing. Conviction is a *feeling*.

> Intention: *"Yeah, I reckon that'd be good to do one day."*
> Conviction: *"I'm going for it."*

See the difference?

Napoleon Hill, author of the self-help classic *Think and Grow Rich*, said:

> There is one quality that one must possess to win, and that is definiteness of purpose, the knowledge of what one wants, and a burning desire to possess it.

Whatever you want, you can't just intellectualise it. It needs to burn in you. You've got to feel it. It's got to give you sweaty palms when you think about it.

What might that be for you?

CONVICTION VS GOALS

Have you ever set a goal, achieved it, and then 'flatlined'? In other words, once the initial euphoria has passed, you're asking yourself, "So now what?"

While they're useful, goals are not enough. Goals are a mechanism to help you narrow in and focus, and to help you measure your progress. But it's the why behind the goal that's more important.

The poet David Whyte says, "What you can plan is too small for you to live." When we look beyond the achievable towards the inspirational, life opens up in front of us.

WHAT MATTERS?

When Steve Jobs was trying to recruit John Scully, then CEO of PepsiCo, to join him at Apple, his provocation was this: "Do you want to spend the rest of your life selling sugared water or do you want a chance to change the world?" How can you argue against that?

Deep down, we all have a desire to do meaningful work. When I worked in the recruitment industry, I found that the main reason people looked to change jobs was that the work they were doing wasn't meaningful. The most effective Change Makers tap a deeper sense of purpose behind all of their efforts.

You want to hold yourself accountable to something great. What are you willing to give up to make way for what matters more?

....

CONVICTION HELPS US FIND
THE ENERGY AND COURAGE TO
DO WHAT IT TAKES WHEN THE
STAKES ARE HIGH.

LEAF IN THE WIND OR ROOTS IN THE GROUND?

Effort and courage are not enough without purpose and direction.

JOHN F. KENNEDY

Why does conviction matter so much to making change happen? Four reasons:

1. YOU'RE GROUNDED

If you were asked, "What do you stand for?", how fluently could you respond?

In my experience, this is a common challenge. Too many people in leadership roles don't know what they stand for, or can't articulate it. What we end up getting is people who can't, or don't, challenge the status quo, so they don't help us move towards a better future. Or, worse, they allow stuff to happen that shouldn't happen. That's not Change Maker behaviour.

In interesting times, things get swirly. When we can't necessarily predict the future based on the past, where do we turn? When we can't rely on traditional authority figures to give us the answers, who do we turn to? When we're looking for truth in a world full of multiple truths, where do we look?

The answer is ourselves.

When the environment around us is swirling with change, choices, and opportunities, conviction gives us roots in the ground to help us stand firm. As the saying goes, if you don't stand for something, you'll stand for anything. When we make a stand for what we deeply believe in, we're less at risk of being buffeted around by the forces at play.

In the not-so-distant past, I got feedback that some people around me didn't know what I stood for. Ouch. No one wants to get feedback like that, especially when you're in a leadership role. It would have been so easy for me to get defensive and make it their problem. But I sat with the feedback for a while, and I realised that perhaps I'd lost touch with what I really stood for, and that was showing up in how I behaved.

2. YOU'RE REAL

The world is crying out for real, relatable leaders. If you want to change things, get real. When you voice what you truly stand for, the world listens.

Here's a way of thinking about that:

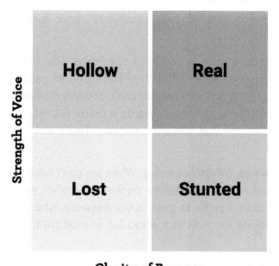

Clarity of Purpose

We need to know our purpose, and we need the conviction to speak it.

If you don't know what you're about, and you don't have a voice, well, you're just plain lost.

If you've got a voice, but it doesn't reflect what you really stand for, it's kind of hollow. You often see these people who swing their weight around in meetings, but don't really have much useful to say.

If you've got a sense of what you're about, but don't have the courage or conviction to put it out there, the world's missing out. And you're stunted. Like the horse in the too-small paddock.

WHEN YOU HAVE CLARITY OF PURPOSE, AND A STRONG VOICE, YOU'RE UNSTOPPABLE.

You're real, and people want a piece of that. You stand by your convictions and influence people with your message.

Cover bands don't change the world. The best songs are the originals. We love the musicians who sing from the heart, and whose music resonates with us. We need leaders who have something heartfelt and authentic to say. They are the catalysts to help us change the world.

3. YOU HAVE A GREATER CHANCE OF MAKING THE IMPACT YOU WANT TO MAKE

Interesting times create opportunities.

They also create leadership vacuums. Vacuums that you can step into. Vacuums that you can create impact from.

Remember: You cannot *not* make an impact.

You have more impact than you might think. So what impact do you want to have?

When you have conviction, that gives you the answer you're looking for.

4. YOU BUILD A TRIBE

If you want to build a ship, don't drum up people to collect wood and don't assign them tasks and work, but rather teach them to long for the endless immensity of the sea.

ANTOINE DE SAINT-EXUPERY

If you want to make change happen, you'll need a tribe. A tribe of people that believe in what you believe in.

Tribes form around people with purpose and conviction.

People are yearning for purpose and meaning in their work right now. In a survey conducted on purpose at work by LinkedIn in 2018, only 30% of people report a sense of meaning or purpose in their work. With a declining level of trust in leadership, and organisations in general, the people and places that stand out are the ones that offer a sense of purpose.

And when they do, they thrive. According to research outlined in the book *Corporate Culture and Performance*, by John Kotter and James Heskett, purpose-driven organisations outperform others by a factor of 12:1. In EY's 2018 report on *The Business Case for Purpose*, they find that "purpose-driven companies make more money, have more engaged employees, more loyal customers, and are even better at innovation and transformational change".

There's clearly something to be said for what happens when you gather people around a common conviction and purpose.

What are you building that others want to be a part of?

The most important thing you can do that will shift you from Seeker to Player, and from Reactive to Creative, is to cultivate a strong sense of conviction.

If you don't stand for something, you'll stand for anything. So you might as well decide what you're about.

WHEN YOU HAVE CLARITY OF
PURPOSE, AND A STRONG VOICE,
YOU'RE UNSTOPPABLE.

HOW TO CULTIVATE CONVICTION

Before you tell your life what you intend to do with it, listen for what it intends to do with you. Before you tell your life what truths and values you have decided to live up to, let your life tell you what truths you embody, what values you represent.

PARKER J. PALMER

How can you kindle the flame of conviction and keep it burning? Here are some practical tools to help you.

1. REFLECTION: CONNECT THE DOTS

You can't connect the dots looking forward; you can only connect them looking backwards.

STEVE JOBS

What does your experience tell you about what you stand for?

We've made choices all our lives. Life throws us situations, and we choose how we respond to them. Sometimes, those experiences are awesome, and we feel truly alive. Other times, they're harder and darker.

If we reflect on our past experiences, we can connect the dots and find some themes about what matters to us. Here's how to get some nuggets of insight:

1. Draw a timeline that looks like this:

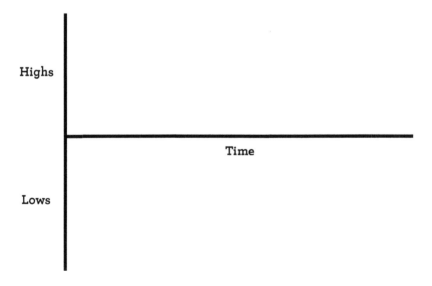

2. Plot the pivotal moments or experiences in your life (growing up, education, travel, career etc.). Include both the highs and the lows (add X's to the timeline and join with lines).

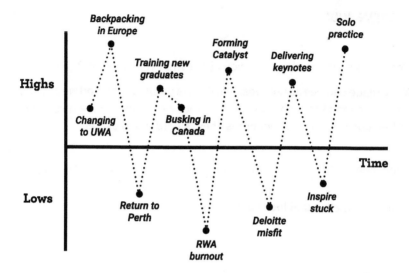

3. Reflect on the 'highs' – your moments of 'aliveness'. What was going on for you then? What caused you to create that situation for yourself? What strengths were you playing to? What was that all about for you? Make some notes about those.

4. Do a similar thing for the 'lows' – your moments of 'darkness'. What was going on for you then? What was missing for you that made it a 'low' rather than a high? What did those times teach you? Make some notes about those.

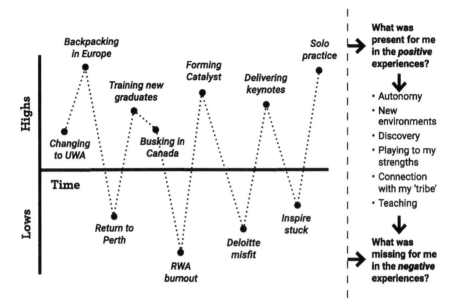

5. Go back over your notes from your highs and lows. What do your life experiences tell you about:

a. what brings you most alive?

b. what your greatest strengths are?

c. what drives you?

6. Finally, step back. What have these experiences been telling you about what you are all about and what you stand for? Write down six words that sum up what you stand for.

	Situation	**Insights**
Highs		
Lows		

Six words that sum up what I stand for:

1.

2.

3.

4.

5.

6.

2. ATTENTION: LISTEN AND LEARN

It did not matter what we expected from life, but rather what life expected from us. We needed to stop asking about the meaning of life but instead to think of ourselves as those who were being questioned by life, daily and hourly.

VIKTOR FRANKL

Another way to tap your conviction is to notice what life is asking of you now. How is it calling to you? When you slow down for a minute, what do you notice? Clarity comes when you let the sediment settle.

Observe the present. Most of us are so caught up in ruminating about the past or anticipating the future that we miss what's happening right now.

Here are some questions to ask yourself:

- **What makes me angry?**
  This is a great question from Neil Crofts, who wrote a paper called *Living on Purpose*. What makes you angry is a clue to what you care deeply about. For example, if you get angry about politicians blaming others, it might mean you care deeply about people taking responsibility for their choices. What makes you angry?

- **What am I great at?**
  Build a legacy from your strengths. In his book *So Good They Can't Ignore You*, Cal Newport suggests that you shouldn't look for your passion. Instead, get so good at something that you become passionate about it. What do you find easy and enjoyable that others say you're awesome at? As management guru Charles Handy says, "Do your best at what you're best at for the benefit of others."

A useful exercise to help you understand what you're great at is to ask others who see you in action. Here are five questions you can ask them:

1. What's the first thing you think of when you think of me?
2. When have you seen me at my best?
3. What do you think are my greatest strengths?
4. What do you think are my greatest accomplishments?
5. How have I made a difference to you?

For a more detailed description of this activity, visit https://bit.ly/2Xtr2CM

- **What gives me sweaty palms?**
  'Sweaty palm moments' are those times when your heart rate cranks up, you're excited and you can't wait to get into it. It's what you're made for. And when you think about it afterwards, you go into that state all over again.

- **What am I holding back on?**
  There are some things that we yearn to do, but we don't. We have one foot on the accelerator and one on the brake. We're torn between doing what's important, and what's safe. And it gnaws at us. That's a clue about what, deep down, the bigger version of ourselves wants to have happen. What are you holding back from doing?

Your answers to these activities will result in certain themes. There'll be a common thread that will point to what matters most to you.

One of the most powerful ways to observe is to use a journal. You could simply write a daily journal reflecting on these questions – either at the beginning of the day or the end. Then, once a month, read over your notes to spot the themes.

3. INTENTION: FOCUS AND CREATE

No leader sets out to be a leader per se, but rather to express him/herself freely and fully.

WARREN BENNIS

Your conviction is not actually what you want for yourself. It's what you want for the world.

Change Makers are naturally future-focused. While it's important to reflect on the past and pay attention to the present, Change Makers obsess about creating a better future.

A powerful exercise to help with this is to define your Big Question.

Your Big Question:
- Creates a massive possibility to live into.
- Reflects your deep conviction.
- Pulls you forward and forces you to grow.
- Provides a foundation for the other three C's (curiosity, connection, and courage).
- Helps you to create more change than you ever imagined possible.

Here are some examples of Change Makers' Big Questions:
- What if people took complete responsibility for the situations they find themselves in, and for shaping their lives? How can we create a culture where that mindset is the norm?
- How can I be part of putting people at the heart of our economic systems?
- How can I help to create spaces for people to thrive?

Your Big Question should have some 'TISA' factors:

1. **Thriller factor:** Should be both scary and exciting to contemplate. It's compelling and spooky like a good thriller.

2. **Intractable factor:** It's potentially paradoxical or seemingly intractable in nature.

3. **Stretch factor:** It will require you to grow, personally and professionally, to meet its challenge.

4. **Ambiguity factor:** You aren't exactly sure how you're going to answer the call of the question.

NOW QUESTIONS

Your Big Question is not the same as your Now Questions. Now Questions are more immediate. They're more of a problem to be solved today rather than a possibility to live into. They're also typically more inwardly 'I' focused rather than externally focused. Now Questions are important but they're not the long game that you're playing.

Examples of Now Questions include:

- How can I influence my boss to get behind this initiative?
- How can I find more time for this project?
- How can I build a network of collaborators?

How to Craft Your Big Question

Here are some tips for crafting your Big Question:

- Listen for what you can't let go of.
- Your Big Question isn't about you. It's about something bigger than you.
- Start the question with a 'What if?' or 'How can we?'
- Draft it, and explain it to someone you don't know very well. Ask for their feedback.
- Now explain it to someone who knows you well. Ask for their feedback.

Your Big Question will likely change over time. In the early stages of exploration it will probably change rapidly, and then once you 'lock on' you'll feel it'll be solid for a while.

Big questions are the result of deep thinking and ongoing reflection. The hard work is here. It should be an uncomfortable and confusing process. Stick with it.

MY BIG QUESTION
Passion: What lights me up?

....

....

....

....

....

....

....

....

....

....

....

....

....

....

Frustration: What makes me angry?

....

....

....

....

....

....

....

....

....

....

....

....

....

....

Vision: What do I want to see happen in the world?

....

....

....

....

....

....

....

....

....

....

....

....

....

....

....

Agency: What's my part in creating that vision?

....

....

....

....

....

....

....

....

....

....

....

....

....

....

....

My Big Question is:

....

....

....

....

....

....

....

....

....

....

IF CONVICTION IS OUR FUEL,
THEN CURIOSITY IS THE
CATALYST.

LIFE TASTES BETTER WITH CONVICTION

One man with conviction will overwhelm a hundred who have only opinions.

WINSTON CHURCHILL

When you have strong conviction, you have more:

- **Clarity:** Your priorities are clearer. Your decisions are that much easier. There's less fog and a better view.
- **Magnetism:** You attract others. If you care about what they care about, they'll care about what you care about. You're onto it when whatever you're on about means something to you and something to others.
- **Courage:** Fear shrinks into the background a little more and you're more likely to act boldly and decisively. You harbour the absolute belief that you're doing the right thing.
- **Authenticity:** You get more done with less drama and you're in flow more often.
- **Progress:** You keep moving. You navigate the turbulence better.

Change Makers who are true to their conviction become the centre of successful change efforts. They make the future.

WHAT HAPPENS WHEN YOU SHOW UP ON PURPOSE?

I went to Fiji for a week to write the initial parts of this book. I stayed in a small, low-key resort right on the beach in front of a great surf break. Imagine elegant palm trees strung with hammocks overlooking a turquoise sea swinging gently in the warm breeze. Yep, it was all there. It would have been all too easy to be lured by all of that, and fritter away the days surfing, eating, and lazing about.

But that didn't happen. I went with a clear purpose, and a goal to achieve. It was all about the book. On the plane on the way there, I drew up a rough daily schedule that included surfing time and siesta time, but the bulk of each day was planned for writing and research.

During my stay, I noticed an interesting dynamic at play, which I suspect was a result of my being so intentional:

- It was easier for me to say no to the less important stuff. I have an inbuilt desire to connect with people. I'm someone who's easily lured into chatting to anyone about anything. By having a clear purpose for my limited time, the pull of the book was stronger than the need for chatter. As a result, it was easier to cut a conversation short and let people know that I was off to continue writing.

- The conversations I did have were somehow more rich and meaningful than merely idle chatter. After my week, I left feeling that I'd established a handful of wonderful new friendships based on some deep and common interests. And I got some great new ideas for the book too!

- Rather than being 'just another tourist passing through', I became known by the staff and guests as 'the guy who's writing a book'. I had people whom I'd never met coming up to me asking, "How's the book going?" I stood out from the crowd without trying to stand out from the crowd.

- Overall, my time there felt unhurried, meaningful, and hugely fulfilling.

I went to Fiji with a 'self-authoring' mindset. (Pardon the pun.) That helped me to be less hidebound by rules and 'what others think'. I was more focused on creating what I really wanted to create.

And it happened because I showed up 'on purpose.'

CHAPTER FIVE: CURIOSITY

LEARN TO SEE THE WATER

Let's just say I was testing the bounds of reality. I was curious to see what would happen. That's all it was: curiosity.

JIM MORRISON

The late novelist David Foster Wallace tells a wonderful story about 'incuriosity' in his commencement speech *This Is Water*:

> There are these two young fish swimming along, and they happen to meet an older fish swimming the other way, who nods at them and says, "Morning, boys, how's the water?" And the two young fish swim on for a bit, and then eventually one of them looks over at the other and goes, "What the hell is water?"

We can all be blind, at times, to the world around us. We might think we know how stuff works, what drives people, that we've got the solution to the problems. But do we really?

A human resources professional I once worked with was tasked with helping the senior leaders of their organisation to have better and more frequent 'talent conversations' with their people. Convinced of the value of this activity, she spent months developing easy-to-use tools and frameworks to help the leaders. But she struggled to get any traction. It took another few months of trying to adapt the tools to make them even better, until she finally asked: "Wait a minute, do these leaders even *want* to have talent conversations?"

The answer was a resounding 'no'. She had assumed that the leaders were keen, but in fact, they were terrified. Not because they didn't know how, but because they saw the conversations with these ambitious people as creating a threat to their own job security.

This is a case of not seeing the water you're swimming in. When you're so close to your own perceptions of how the world works, you can forget to ask the bigger questions that really matter. Knowledge overwhelms curiosity.

YOU CAN'T KNOW EVERYTHING (BUT TRY ANYWAY)

Curiosity is the driving force behind creativity, innovation, and change. It's been the seed of change, forever.

If conviction is our fuel, then curiosity is the catalyst.

It's the spark that ignites the engine to take us into new territory.

LEARNING TO KNOW

Unlike fish, we're born with an innate sense of curiosity. When we're at our most human, we've got a strong desire to know. We're wired to ask why. Early in life, we're a blank slate. The neurons in our brain are largely free-floating, waiting to be connected in ways that help us make sense of the world. The world's a mystery, waiting to be explored. Research by the Right Question Institute, a non-profit organisation concerned with teaching people to ask the right questions, shows us that as young kids, we ask up to 300 questions per day.

As we grow older, we can be like the two young fish in the story. By the time we reach the age of 15, we're down to asking almost no questions. (For more on the research, check out https://bit.ly/2G8st46)

As we accumulate knowledge about ourselves, others, and the world, we can begin to cruise on autopilot. We've begun to work out how stuff works, and the way things are. Our brains, once a mass of billions of unconnected neurons, have created neural pathways that enable us to do things without, as Nobel Prize winner Daniel Kahneman calls it, *cognitive strain*. Our brains, quite simply, just want to use as little energy as possible.

But when we forget to ask questions about *why* things are the way they are, and assume that 'the way things are is the way things are', we can get into trouble. And never has that been truer than now, when 'the way things are' seems to be challenged in all sorts of domains.

LEARNING TO ASK

Curiosity happens when there's a gap between what you know and what you think could be known.

The more you know, the more you realise there is to know. Until you think there isn't. Some people, in their pursuit of knowledge, reach a point where they think they know it all, and lose their curiosity.

There's a correlation between the amount of knowledge you think you have and the amount of curiosity you demonstrate. *Wired* magazine published an article called 'The Itch of Curiosity', highlighting research on curiosity that used functional magnetic resonance imaging (fMRI). The results of that research suggests the correlation looks like this:

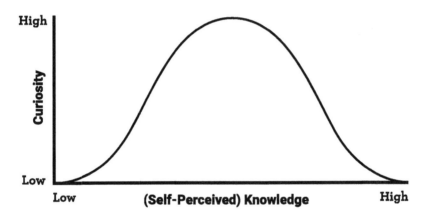

In other words, when there's a gap between what you think you know, and what you think could be known, you're curious.

Let's break it down a little more:

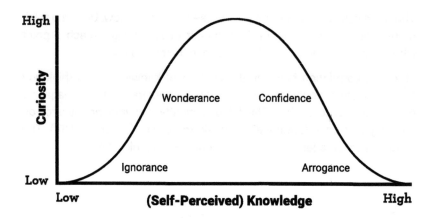

When you have no knowledge of something, there's nothing to be curious about. Think of the young fish in the water. That's ignorance.

When the old fish swims by, you start to get curious. What's he talking about? That's wonderance.

When you realise you've actually learned something new, when you 'see the water', you can apply that knowledge to your world. That's confidence.

If you think you know everything, you think there's nothing to be curious about. You know it all, right? That's arrogance.

There's a tipping point somewhere between ignorance and wonderance. It's a bit like sex. When you don't know what you don't know, you're not so interested (think pre-teen). When it's on tap, you're not so interested either. When you've had a taste, and want more, it's an insatiable hunger.

The peak of curiosity is where we have some knowledge but not too much. Studies show that when we're given a little information that piques our curiosity, we want to know more. There's a gap between what we know and what we want to know.

That's what makes a good thriller movie so compelling – we're on the edge of our seats, wanting to know what's going to happen next. Once we get to a point where we think we know enough, our curiosity to know more declines.

In a world that values answers, it's tempting to rush towards the right-hand end. Ryan Holiday, the author of *The Obstacle Is the Way*, says when your ego gets bigger than your ears, your curiosity starts to die. When people keep calling you Superman, soon enough you start to believe you are.

KNOWING *AND* ASKING

The trick is to stay curious at all times.

To stay in that place between wonderance and confidence. Know what you know. Be humble about it. In a world where yesterday's solutions are less effective at solving today's problems, those who can stay curious will help us create new ways forward.

Transportation expert Wanis Kabbaj is a good example. In his TED talk, he explains how he's been trying to solve the increasingly huge traffic problems that rapid urbanisation presents us with. He asked: "What if traffic flowed through our streets as smoothly and efficiently as blood flows through our veins?" By simply asking that question, and being in 'wonderance', he's taken our thinking in a new direction that just might yield new solutions.

A CEO client of mine makes a habit of looking for 'disconfirming data'. That's the stuff that goes against your closely held beliefs. He believes that if you're not looking for disconfirming data, you're missing the whole picture. The movie *The Big Short* is about a small group of people who looked for, and found, disconfirming data during the subprime mortgage market bubble during 2007–2010. Ninety-nine percent of the market did not see that the bubble was going to burst. This small group saw what others refused to see, and when the market crashed, they were ready.

As Change Makers, we need to be confident that we know stuff. In large part, that's what we're paid for. At the same time, we need to be curious too. The challenge is to not be ignorant, but not be arrogant either. Either end is where the traps are. We need to balance confidence (relying on what we know) with wonderance (knowing that we don't know it all, and seeking out answers). That's the learning zone.

....

THE MORE YOU KNOW, THE
MORE YOU REALISE THERE IS
TO KNOW. UNTIL YOU THINK
THERE ISN'T.

YOU'VE GOTTA KEEP LEARNING

You can't see the whole sky through a bamboo tube.

JAPANESE PROVERB

The more curious we are, the more likely we are to adapt and thrive.

Scientists and historians believe that one of the main reasons the Neanderthals became extinct and our *Sapiens* species survived is because Sapiens was the more curious of the two. We kept exploring and adapting. As Yuval Noah Harari, author of *Sapiens*, puts it:

> *Sapiens did not forage only for food and materials. They foraged for knowledge as well. To survive, they needed a detailed mental map of their territory. To maximise the efficiency of their daily search for food, they required information about the growth patterns of each plant and the habits of each animal. They needed to know which foods were nourishing, which made you sick, and how to use others as cures. They needed to know the progress of the seasons and what warning signs preceded a thunderstorm or a dry spell. They studied every stream, every walnut tree, every bear cave, and every flint-stone deposit in their vicinity.*

Roll forward a few millennia, and curiosity is just as important now. We live in interesting times. It's fair to say that the world we live in is ever-changing, and when the past isn't necessarily a reliable predictor of the future anymore, we need to get curious about finding new ways to solve the problems we face, and to find new and different ways to create what we want.

Curiosity is on the rise:

- Michael Dell, the chief executive of Dell, Inc., believes that curiosity is the number one attribute CEOs will need most to succeed in the turbulent times ahead.

- The World Economic Forum's 2018 report *Towards a Reskilling Revolution* highlights the shift required in our current global context: "What will be required is nothing less than a societal mindset shift for people to become creative, curious, agile lifelong learners, comfortable with continuous change."

- A Fast Company report asserts that in a world of automation, curiosity is one of the four uniquely human skills (along with contextualisation, critical thinking, and ethical judgement) that will be in increasing demand. It's something that robots will never be able to replace.
- In organisations the world over, curiosity is becoming prized as a quality sought after in new hires and existing employees alike. Companies such as Microsoft, Infosys, and Google would rather hire people who have a high 'learning quotient', train them, and have them leave, than hire people who aren't curious and don't learn.

HOW TO DIAL UP YOUR CURIOSITY

It's not what you look at that matters, it's what you see.

HENRY DAVID THOREAU

My guess is that you're already naturally curious. Let's look at how you can dial it up even more.

Let's use three lenses on curiosity:

1. Yourself (self-awareness)
2. Other people (empathy)
3. The wider world (perspective)

The first is 'attention in'. The second and third are 'attention out'. That proportion – one third to two thirds – is a sensible balance to help keep things in proportion. Too much attention in? That's just self-indulgent. Too much attention out? That's lacking self-awareness and self-esteem.

YOURSELF

The place to start is to be curious about yourself. As the saying goes on the temple at Delphi, "Know thyself." One of the 20th century's most revered management gurus, Peter Drucker, wrote the classic *Harvard Business Review* article 'Managing Oneself'. His premise is that an age of unprecedented opportunity brings unprecedented responsibility. We need to chart our own courses, and that means we need to know the vessel we are the captain of. If we are to thrive, we need to cultivate a deep understanding of how we're wired. We need to be deeply curious about ourselves.

Curiosity brings awareness. And awareness brings choice. When we have greater self-awareness, we can get off autopilot and into making more deliberate choices. We're able to stand back from ourselves and go, "Interesting. There I go again, talking over the top of people. Perhaps for this next five minutes I'll choose to listen more than I talk." And so the process of learning and growth is enhanced.

Drucker suggests we dwell on questions such as "What are my strengths?", "How do I work?", "What are my values?", "Where do I belong?", and "What can I contribute?" They're all powerful avenues to explore, and play right into the exercises in the previous chapter on Conviction.

Here are some other questions you can get in the habit of asking yourself:

- What's driving me right now?
- How might I be coming across?
- How did I come to that conclusion?
- How might I be wrong?
- What do I want?
- Why do I want it?
- What am I afraid of?
- What have I learned today?

OTHERS

David Foster Wallace once said that there is no experience you've had that you are not the absolute centre of. If we let ourselves think that we're the centre of the world, we're in for a tough ride. It's long been a principle of counsellors and therapists that fostering a curiosity about others can free people from hard-wired self-obsession and judgement.

Wallace gives a great example of being in a long, slow-moving line at the supermarket checkout, standing behind a lady screaming at her three-year-old child. You might write her off as a loser who lacks the parenting skills to manage her kid in public.

Or, if you're aware and curious enough, you might imagine that perhaps she's had no sleep for the past three nights, holding the hand of her husband who's dying of bone cancer. Stop your autopilot thinking and try to connect with another person's world, even if it's just in your own mind. That discipline gives you the chance to create a new perspective, which can lead to different choices.

One way to develop a greater curiosity about others is to simply *observe*.

When you deliberately observe what's going on, you create an opportunity to see more of the whole.

Here are some things you can do to strengthen your curiosity towards others:

- Get to your next café meeting 10 minutes early. Sit quietly and observe the interactions between people. Imagine what it might be like to be one of them.
- Watch a movie with the sound turned down and notice the actors' facial expressions and body language. Imagine what they're aiming to express.

In each case, notice what you notice. Write it down. You'll likely discover a distinction between what you see and the stories you tell yourself about what you see.

A few years ago, as part of a course I was doing, one of my assignments was to observe people interacting every day. I needed to write down a) what I noticed and b) what I made up in my head about what I noticed. It was useful to discern the difference. If I noticed an animated conversation between a group of surfers on the beach, my imagination went to thinking that they were having an argument about who dropped in on whom. But it could have just as well been a conversation about the shark one of them saw in the line-up. Who was I to say what it was about?

CURIOSITY BRINGS AWARENESS. AND AWARENESS BRINGS CHOICE.

THE WORLD

As much as you might like it to, your willpower alone won't change things. It's smart to learn to see and harness the bigger forces at play in the world, so you have a more accurate map of the 'maze'.

One of my favourite movies is *Surf's Up*. It's about a penguin wannabe surfer, Cody Maverick, who finds himself in the thick of the action at a world surf contest. He gets himself a mentor in Big Z, a legend of surfing in days gone by. Big Z has some wisdom for Cody:

> *You let the wave do the work. You don't fight the wave. You can't fight these big waves.*

Head to any surfing beach and you'll see this in action. Experienced surfers won't rush out there. They'll spend time on the beach observing the patterns of the waves, the currents, and the tides before heading out. In the water, they're the ones who make it look effortless. Using their understanding of the patterns at play, they'll always be in the right position, letting the wave come to them, and using the wave's energy to generate huge board speed with minimal effort. Less experienced surfers will more likely miss the nuances of the patterns. They might get waves, but it'll be harder work.

It's a metaphor for all arenas. Your organisation, your industry, society, culture: they are all 'big waves' in a complex system with their own direction and powerful energy. Trying to change them with brute force doesn't work. You can't fight these big waves.

But what you *can* do is learn to see how they work. The patterns at play. The predominant thinking. The trends. And you can deliberately work *with* those forces to do your thing.

Here's an example. One of my clients is a fairly hierarchical, process-bound, government agency. My role is to bring fresh thinking and new ways of doing things in the leadership development space. The idea being that some outside perspective is a good thing. It's also fraught with potential difficulty, with the possible clash between my ideas and their current ways of doing things.

How do I make that work? Well, I don't have the luxury to 'stand on the beach' and wander around and get to know the culture – they aren't paying me for that. And diving straight in could end in tears.

Instead, I do my work by thinking about two aspects at the same time:

- **Task:** The first is the 'task' lens – in this case, to design and deliver a leadership development programme with the client. In the surfing metaphor, that would be to 'catch some waves'. That's what I'm there for.

- **Patterns:** The second is the 'patterns' lens. As I do the 'task' work, I'm acutely listening and looking for signs that tell me about the culture, the ways of working, the predominant thinking in the organisation. I'll test my ideas and observe how people respond. I'll notice where ideas get traction, and where they hit roadblocks.

Here are some 'patterns' questions for you to ask as you go about your day-to-day work:

- What are the forces at play that influence what people choose to do and say, or not do and say?

- Under what conditions do things seem to flow easily, where work just gets done? Under what conditions does the opposite happen?

- What are the rules of the game here? What assumptions or beliefs do people hold that influence their behaviours?

- What are the 'no-go areas' – the lines that shall not be crossed?

Listen for words, look for body language. Notice what you notice. Write it down. Stand back from your thoughts and look for the patterns. Over time, with practice, you'll develop an instinct for it. And you'll be better positioned to make change in your own turbulent arena.

Here are four more ways to dial up your curiosity:

1. Expand your experience.

Get yourself out of your comfort zone. Seek surprise. Walk a different way to work. Hang out with people who think differently to you. Visit a new country each year. Create serendipitous moments.

2. Expand your mind.

Go to a physical bookshop or a library. Don't go to your usual favourite section. If you like science, go to the poetry section. Pick up a random book from there, choose a page and start reading. Don't stop for 5 minutes. Notice what grabs your attention. Rinse and repeat.

3. Ask different questions.

Be like Wanis Kabbaj. Make your default questions broad and open-ended, like "Why?" and "What if?" Sound like your three-year-old self.

4. Cultivate 'beginner's mind'.

Learn something completely new. That could be a new language, a new skill, a new sport. Be willing to be wrong, to look like a kook, to experience the pure joy of learning something new.

AS MUCH AS YOU MIGHT LIKE
IT TO, YOUR WILLPOWER ALONE
WON'T CHANGE THINGS.

SEE DIFFERENT, ACT DIFFERENT

The important thing is to not stop questioning.
Curiosity has its own reason for existing.

ALBERT EINSTEIN

Curiosity is a powerful tool in the Change Maker's toolkit. When you dial up your curiosity:

1. **You find signals in the noise, and it's easier to join the dots.**
   When you're curious, you see things that others don't. You discern patterns that lead to new insights. And you find new pathways that lead to new possibilities.

2. **You stay smarter, longer.**
   People who make a lifelong habit of reading and writing slow their mental rate of decline by a third compared to those who only did an average amount of those things. In her article 'An Active Brain Throughout Life Slows Cognitive Decline', researcher Sue Hughes describes a study which found that older people who rarely read or wrote experienced a cognitive decline that was 48% faster compared to the average.

3. **You stay relevant and valuable.**
   It's estimated that between 40% and 60% of roles (including professional ones) will be significantly affected in the near-term by the impact of robotics and artificial intelligence. Curiosity is a uniquely human trait. The ability to stay curious keeps you learning and keeps you relevant.

4. **You're more able to handle change when it happens.**
   If you act on your curiosity time and time again, you're getting more familiar with the new and the different. In other words, you're becoming friends with change rather than seeing it as the enemy. So when that big gnarly unexpected change comes out of left field, you're ready.

5. You make change happen.
When you cultivate your insatiable curiosity, you keep the world evolving. You become one of the people who challenge the status quo. You generate different perspectives for the benefit of us all, and invent new ways. Curiosity is the catalyst of innovation, and a gift for a better world.

CHAPTER SIX: CONNECTION

The strongest drug that exists for a human is another human being.

ANON

ALL FIRED UP

While I was in Fiji to write this book, I met some interesting characters. One of them was a fellow called James, who is an expert in rehabilitating coral reefs. For the past three years he had been coming to Fiji from the UK for a few months to help the locals re-establish the dying coral reef systems on the south coast of the main island.

James's work was voluntary. He was doing it because he held a strong conviction for the importance of healthy reef systems and was dismayed to see the state of the coral there. What most people would imagine would be pristine, colourful ecosystems were in fact nothing of the sort. They were polluted with plastic and struggling to survive. It was a worthy cause. He was on a mission to make a difference.

Early during my time there, he visited some of the coral farms he'd set up the year before and taught the locals how to cultivate. Disappointingly, the coral farms had been pretty much forgotten about, and all his good work from the year before had seemingly come to nothing.

Frustrated, he spent time visiting the local villagers to try to educate them on the importance of looking after the coral farms. He lectured them on how much waste they were putting into the ocean and the negative effect it was having. He reminded them about the good work they had done in years past, and endeavoured to re-educate them on the techniques they'd let lapse.

Each night, he'd come back to where we were staying and tear his hair out, exasperated that they didn't seem to get it. He talked of seeing the nodding heads, and hearing the exuberant yeses that the locals knew he wanted to hear, but in his heart, he knew they weren't on board. What was he missing?

Some months after I left, I got a message from James:

Digby, I've learned a valuable lesson these past few months. I used to think that to make change happen in the communities, all they needed was expertise. And I could give them that. But you know what? Expertise is only one little thing. What they needed was the collective willpower to do something about it. And my evangelistic approach didn't help make that happen.

One of the locals eventually found the courage to sit down with me and let me know that people were getting frustrated with me showing up, and that I needed to back off. So, I did that, and just went diving for a few weeks. And you know what? After that he came back to me and said they'd like me to join them in a conversation about what to do about the reefs. But on the condition that I wasn't allowed to tell them what to do. I was just another voice in the conversation.

Man, that was an experience. They all have a voice. They listen to each other even though they might not agree. It seems they look for the common denominator about what's most important to everyone. There was so much laughter too! I kind of learned that to them, connection comes first.

So, where things are at now, is that I'm still around to help them, but they're leading it. Which is what I wanted in the first place. But my job is to help them when they need it, not to tell them what to do all the time. It's kind of liberating!

CONNECTION IS YOUR BRIDGE

If you want to go fast, go alone. If you want to go far, go together.

AFRICAN PROVERB

Connection is your bridge between your ideas and the impact you want to make.

How you connect to others matters.

In James's story, it seems to me that what he was missing wasn't conviction. He had plenty of that. What he was missing was the ability to see and create connections with others in ways that helped his change-making agenda get traction.

Conviction is important, but it isn't enough. Change Making is also about your ability to connect deeply with people, and help others connect together, to get ideas to take root and spread.

Connection is a primal need. It's a fundamental part of being human. Since the mid-20th century, Abraham Maslow's hierarchy of needs has provided us with a useful way of prioritising our human needs. Belonging and connecting – the need for relationships – is in the middle of the hierarchy, below esteem and self-actualisation, and above physiological and safety needs. It makes intuitive sense – the human brain is driven by a basic instinct to survive, and getting these fundamental needs met should trump all others. Right?

···

CONNECTION IS A PRIMAL NEED.

Maslow's Hierarchy of Needs

Recent research in neuroscience shows us that *none* of Maslow's hierarchy of needs can be met without social connection. We've survived as a species because we have learned to connect and collaborate with each other. In his book *Social: Why Our Brains Are Wired to Connect*, neuroscientist Dr. Matthew Lieberman suggests that as babies, we couldn't get access to other fundamentals – food, water, and shelter – without being able to make some sort of connection with others who could provide it. We connect to get our needs met. It's our fundamental driving force.

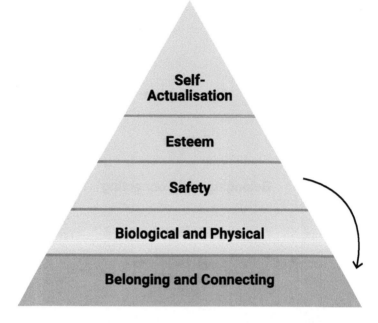

A revised version of Maslow's Hierarchy of Needs

Societies and organisations are nothing if not a network of people in relationship with each other. Connection is about the ability to foster relationships between yourself and others, as well as to foster relationships between people. In other words, to create change, you need to connect.

CONNECTIONS ARE THE CATALYST

Never doubt that a small group of thoughtful, committed citizens can change the world; indeed, it's the only thing that ever has.

MARGARET MEAD

If you've ever tried to make change happen though a hierarchy (maybe your own organisation), you've probably experienced the frustration and angst of trying to get the boss's attention, pitching your case for signoff, and waiting an eternity for a decision. Then only to be told, "We need signoff from the next level up" or "It's more complicated than we thought. Can you leave it with me?"

In years past, hierarchy and the processes that came with it worked well when change was relatively linear, and predictability was within reach. In the 21st century, our context has changed, and so our ways of making change happen must also change. In interesting times, making change happen through hierarchy and formal channels is too slow. As management thinker Harold Jarche has eloquently outlined:

> *19th century work got done through artisans; 20th century work got done through hierarchies; 21st century work gets done through networks. The more you are connected, and the better you are able to connect with anyone, the more effective you will be.*

A small number of individuals can influence big change across a system.

Management consultant Leandro Herrero, author of *Viral Change*, identified that the people who tend to be the most connected in an organisation are the ones most likely to influence change. He also found that people are influenced more by their peers than people senior to them, so those Change Makers will likely be in the ranks of the organisation, not at the top.

Social skills such as empathy are increasingly in demand. In 2016, *The Economist* reported that since 1980, growth in employment and pay has been fastest in professions across the income scale that put a high premium on social skills.

CONNECT BETTER

How can you connect better? Let's look at that through the lenses of:

1. **Me** – Build your network
2. **S/He** – Build a bridge
3. **We** – Build a community

ME – *BUILD YOUR NETWORK*

Be around the light bringers, the magic makers, the world shifters, the game shakers.
They challenge you, break you open, uplift and expand you.
They don't let you play small with your life.
These heartbeats are your people.
These people are your tribe.

DANIELLE DOBY

YOU ALREADY HAVE A NETWORK. IS IT THE ONE YOU NEED?

In my experience, most people have some form of network, but it's not usually the one they need, and they don't know how to leverage it.

Your network is simply your tribe. It's the people who are there for you, and you're there for them. It's a mutually beneficial set of relationships.

A diverse network is a strong network. The most effective Change Makers deliberately cultivate and make the most of a reciprocal network of trusted relationships to help them do three things consistently well:

- **Deliver:** Help you get work done.
- **Discover:** Give you new ideas, information, and opportunities.
- **Recover:** Lift your spirit and keep you sane.

Here are nine different types of important network roles:

Network Connection Type	Network Connection Role	Description
Deliver: Help you get work done.	***Trusted Peers***	People who can do the same type of work you do. They can help share the load.
	Able Enablers	People who bring skills and resources that you don't have.
	Savvy Advisors	People who may have done it before, and/or can give you broader context and savvy advice.
Discover: Give you new ideas, information, and opportunities.	***Door Openers***	People who can connect you to new people, opportunities, and possibilities.
	Alt. Thinkers	People who think in different ways to you, bringing fresh ideas and perspectives.
	Critical Friends	People who will give you developmental feedback and challenge you.
Recover: Lift your spirit and keep you sane.	***Wise Guides***	People with whom you can seek wise counsel and insight.
	Good Mates	People with whom you can let off steam and just kick back.
	Solid Grounders	People who help you get a healthy work–life balance.

Take a moment to write down at least one person you know who could fit each role (they can be the same person for different roles).

Network Connection Type	Network Connection Role	Name
Deliver: Help you get work done.	*Trusted Peers*	
	Able Enablers	
	Savvy Advisors	
Discover: Give you new ideas, information, and opportunities.	*Door Openers*	
	Alt. Thinkers	
	Critical Friends	
Recover: Lift your spirit and keep you sane.	*Wise Guides*	
	Good Mates	
	Solid Grounders	

For a more comprehensive network diagnostic experience and tool, go to https://bit.ly/2Enszlo

Some tips for building your network:

- Build bridges before you need them. Invest in relationships not because you need something. Invest in relationships for the sake of them.
- Ensure you have some 'colliding perspectives' in your network – those people who think differently to you and give you fresh perspectives.
- Think 80/20: 20% of the people will be your primary go-to's for most situations. There's a saying "You are the average of the five people you spend the most time with." Make sure those five cover the majority of the network roles.

S/HE – *BUILD A BRIDGE*

Speak in such a way that others love to listen to you.
Listen in such a way that others love to speak to you.

ANON

Make every connection real. Whenever you're in conversation with someone else, you have an opportunity to make a connection. It's the quality of the exchange that matters. As Susan Scott, author of *Fierce Conversations*, says, "The conversation is the relationship."

Let's be clear. A conversation is not just sitting down over coffee. It's any time you're in the process of sharing information and ideas with others. That could be as simple as a text or as big as a keynote presentation. A good idea is to remember that you're basically 'in conversation' when you're in the presence of others.

Your aim in any conversation is to 'build a bridge' between you and them. Here are four ways to do that:

1. Be 'attention out'.

People respond to attention. 'Attention out' is when your attention is on 'the other'. By contrast, 'attention in' is when your attention is primarily on yourself. 'Attention out' shows others that you're genuinely interested in them. Building a bridge becomes easier. People actually appreciate it more, and they feel like they're getting some attention. Silence your ego and allow them to be heard.

2. Be curious.

The person you know most about is you (and that's an ongoing journey). It stands to reason that you know even less about everyone else. You might *think* you know stuff about them, but that's just what you make up, and it might be wildly inaccurate. To build a bridge, stay curious. Listen, question, observe, wonder. With this orientation, you'll both learn and you'll be someone worth being with.

3. Be vulnerable.

You're not perfect, you're human. In our digitally driven world, people yearn for humanity in their connections. There's something hugely powerful about sharing what you find hard, the stuff you haven't got nailed yet. It's an incredibly attractive quality to have as a leader. It endears us to you, and makes you appear as human as the rest of us. We're more willing to follow you and to work with you. Next time you're invited to share something of your story, think about what you could share that you find hard.

4. Be of service.

Ultimately, when you serve another, you will build a stronger relationship. What being of service looks like will depend on what you notice after adopting the other three ways of being above. You might serve by providing some advice. Perhaps you can connect them to someone else that could help them. Maybe you could respectfully challenge their assumptions. Or perhaps just listening well is all it takes.

WE – *BUILD A COMMUNITY*

Peter Block, in his article 'From Leadership to Citizenship', talks about how leaders could be more inclusive. Here's one of his suggestions:

First, we would ask all of them to sit down. There is no need for them to stand up since we will not be watching them so closely. We might ask them to sit with us, to join us. We need their experience, their wisdom, even their direction. It is just not necessary to look up at them.

As a Change Maker, sometimes it's necessary to be centre stage. But increasingly, the rest of us don't want to be talked at. We want to talk *with*. We want a sense of belonging and inclusion. We want to shape something *together*.

Your role as a Change Maker is to **build a community of people who want to go on the journey with you.** They share your conviction, your ideas. Your job is not to be in the centre of all of that. It's to put those ideas at the centre and let others feast on them. Be one *of*, not *the* one.

Some tips to build a community:

1. Be a host.
When you host a party, you invite the guests, create a conducive environment, and as they arrive you help them orientate and settle in. Likewise, be a host for conversations about the ideas you share in common. You don't need to be the one with all the answers. Facilitate. Create experiences for people to participate in. Help meaning and engagement emerge.

2. Be a connector.
Connect people who you think might benefit from knowing each other. Who do you know that could benefit someone else you know? Connect them and get out of the way.

3. Be a reminder.
You can build a community by being the person that reminds others why they're there in the first place. You don't need to be the perfect role model. Just the one who says from time to time, "Hey, remember what we're all about here."

CONNECT AND THRIVE

When you connect powerfully with others, you'll thrive as a Change Maker. **Here are just some of the benefits:**

- Change Making is challenging. Having the right people around you sustains and grows you.
- You'll be known as someone worth spending time with. Those who experience your presence, your interest, and your willingness to invest your interest in them will remember that, and tell others.
- It'll be easier to access fresh and different ideas.
- You'll get more done faster through others.
- Quite simply, you'll be a more powerful Change Maker.

"WE DON'T KNOW"

A few years ago, I worked with managers charged with implementing a new system in a large public sector organisation. They were facing a major business change that would significantly alter their core business processes and help their organisation to be more relevant and agile. Think of it like when banks moved to online banking – it was of a similar magnitude, in the shift in both mindset and process. It was big, complex, and potentially messy.

The process wasn't going to happen overnight, and they were charged with keeping business-as-usual running smoothly while preparing to take themselves, and their teams, successfully through the change. Sound familiar?

Our work together was about helping them to begin to make sense of the changes ahead, to understand their role in it all, and to build the confidence to navigate it successfully.

In various locations around the world, we held a number of three-day workshops. After initial presentations by senior leaders on the 'why' and 'what' of the changes, there were many questions from the managers about the detail of how things were going to work. When would X and Y be rolled out? What can and can't we do? What if Z happens? What will we do then? Understandable questions, to be sure.

For most of these questions, the answer from the senior leaders was: "We don't know. We need you to help us figure it all out. Can we start doing that together now?"

'We don't know' are not words you'd expect from a senior leader. Don't they have it all worked out? Isn't that why they're paid the big bucks? What do you mean, you don't know? Where's the plan?

Of course, with the organisation moving into brand new territory and addressing a challenge like this, no one had all the answers, or even half of them. As with all complex challenges, the answers emerge through trying things out and learning from what happens. It's the collective, connected effort that keeps things moving.

It was refreshing to hear those words: "We don't know." They were authentic, honest, and they helped to create the conditions for new possibilities to emerge. That's connection in action, right there.

Here's the beautiful thing. On the morning of the third day, the managers had got it. To quote one of them:

> *I came in with a huge list of questions I needed answered. Now I know I don't need all the answers. I'm OK with working it out as we go along. I'm going to lead my team to try some new things, see what works, and learn from our experiences. I'm on board.*

CHAPTER SEVEN: COURAGE

Fear is a reaction, courage is a decision.

WINSTON CHURCHILL

THE MOMENT OF COURAGE

The Greatest Showman is a BIG movie. From the word go, it's in your face. It's got big characters, big drama, and a big soundtrack. It exudes an air of confidence: "Watch me!"

The cornerstone song of the movie is called 'This Is Me'. It's sung by Keala Settle, who plays the bearded lady in the circus troupe. Her character's story is one of coming from obscurity, overcoming insecurities, and stepping out to find her voice. And she nails it. It's big. It's inspiring.

But to me, the more powerful story is the one behind the script. There's a less well-known video you can find online of Keala and the cast in rehearsal. In fact, it's not just any rehearsal. It's the 'green light' session where the cast and choir were performing every song to the Hollywood moguls to get the nod to go ahead and make the movie. No pressure.

The clip shows Keala starting off the song, standing behind the lectern, reading the words and looking fairly tentative. She doesn't make much eye contact and her body is relatively rigid. It sounds OK, but it's hardly inspiring.

About a third of the way into the song, something happens. While still singing, she appears to have an idea that perhaps moving the lectern away would be a good idea. As she shifts the physical barrier to the side, her mental and emotional barriers seem to melt away too. She steps boldly out into the centre of the room, faces the choir, and dials it up. She becomes a force, a power, and the whole room lifts with her. You can see it on the faces of the choir – they light up and throw everything into it.

Keala appears to abandon any need for approval. She's embodying 'This Is Me' in every way.

By the end, the room is in tears. Nothing will be the same after that.

And the result? Well, they made the movie!

Here's the link: https://bit.ly/2CaoKgP

. . . .

THERE'S SOMETHING HUGELY POWERFUL ABOUT SHARING WHAT YOU FIND HARD.

DO YOU NEED CONFIDENCE, OR COURAGE?

Courage is one of those qualities that distinguishes the bold from the bland.

But I reckon there's a little trap that people can fall into. One they set themselves up for. Like so many barriers to our own success, it comes down to a choice of words.

That choice is between confidence and courage.

Example: A client says she needs to build up the confidence to put a contentious issue on the table with her executive team. I ask her, "Do you need confidence, or courage?"

What's the difference, you might ask? Surely we're talking semantics? Let me suggest otherwise.

Courage is what you have when you face something scary, and you do it anyway. Confidence is what you have after you've done it.

Courage is a leap of faith. Confidence is backed by experience.

Courage comes from wanting something badly enough that you'll do what it takes. Confidence is knowing you can do it.

Courage shows us we're capable of more than we thought. Confidence sustains us at that new level.

You can have courage without confidence.

Confidence comes from courage.

Confidence

Courage

It's easier to hide behind a lack of confidence, when actually, what you're saying is that you have a lack of courage. If you reframe it so it's about having courage, not confidence, it's a different game you're playing. Courage comes from a deeper place than confidence. One you can tap without having to have been there before.

In a world where we're daily facing new situations without a blueprint, we need more leaders with courage, not just confidence.

So, for your next gnarly challenge, what do you need?

THE SOURCE OF COURAGE

If confidence comes from courage, where does courage come from?

Confidence not earned from courageous deeds is a fragile shell that's easily shattered. We all yearn for a deep, grounded inner confidence, and we want to see it in those who lead us.

So where does courage come from? What allows some people to take bold action in the face of the unknown, while others shrink back and stay safe?

Two answers:

1. Conviction

How much do you want it? Why would you even bother? What makes it worth the risk? You've got to be able to answer those questions with conviction if you're ever going to be able to muster the courage to act decisively.

2. Connection

When you're surrounded by other courageous people, you're more likely to step up. And when you know people have got your back, it gives you the fortitude to step away from safety. Funny how 'encouragement' has the word 'courage' in it...

I'm right into mountain biking. There's a local trail I started riding earlier this year that has one section that used to scare the crap out of me. A series of steep, swooshing drops that you can't do half-heartedly. It's an all-or-nothing affair. The first few times I approached that section I'd get off my bike and walk it, and quietly wonder how anyone could ride it. I eventually convinced myself to 'man up' and stay on the bike. So I'd approach it tentatively, with the brakes on full. What do you think happened? I fell off every time. Oh, the frustration...

Fast-forward a few weeks. I was riding with a friend in front of me. We approached the gnarly section. He didn't slow down, went straight into it, and flew through unscathed. Wow, it's possible! Without thinking too much, and with my heart in my mouth, I followed his line, and all of a sudden I was out the other end with no broken bones. Yee ha! The switch had been flicked. Now I ride that section at full speed, minimal brakes. I actually look forward to it. It's the best part of the trail. I love it.

My courage to tackle that section full-on came from those two C's: conviction (my burning desire to do it) and connection (seeing my friend do it).

That looks like this:

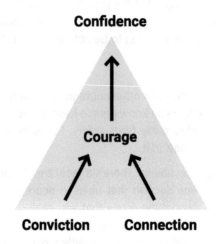

Confidence

Courage

Conviction   **Connection**

NOTHING NEW HAPPENS WITHOUT ACTION.

Change is the result of taking new and different actions. And most of the time, that takes some courage.

Like for Keala Settle, the moment of courage happens when we decide to cross a threshold. Away from certainty and safety, and into vulnerability and possibility.

When we choose courage over certainty, something profound happens to us. Something gets ignited, sometimes quietly, and sometimes earthshakingly. A little more of the person we wish we could be shows up. Sometimes, the person we didn't even know we could be comes alive. And we relish it.

Every day, we're given the opportunity to act on moments of courage. Look for them, listen for them. And then act on them.

YOU ARE AT THE EDGE

Change happens at the edge of things. The edge between the known and the unknown. In our complex world, old ways of operating are less likely to serve us now. The time is ripe for inventing new ways. Be at the edge where the new can grow out from the old. Courage can take you there, and keep you there, thriving.

At the edge is where we more often than not find ourselves in life these days, whether we like it or not. Interesting times can take us inevitably towards the edge of our own comfort zones, presenting us with a choice. Do we stay safe, or do we lean into what life is asking of us, and towards what we know deep down that we really want? The edge of the threshold is always there.

And that's where the learning is too. A mentor of mine, Kim Lisson, used to tell me, "Look for the discomfort. The learning's nearby." You'll know from experience that your greatest growth comes from overcoming discomfort and difficulty. There's plenty of research to back your instincts up.

For example, for their book *Geeks and Geezers*, leadership researchers Warren Bennis and Rob Thomas interviewed more than 40 top leaders from all walks of life and found that all of them had a number of 'crucible moments': intense experiences that severely tested them, forcing them to question who they were and what mattered to them. And, for over 30 years, the Centre for Creative Leadership has found that leaders with the greatest 'developmental advantage' are the ones who have learned to 'love the heat' and live at the edge. (For more on this, check out Nick Petrie's whitepaper *Future Trends in Leadership Development* at https://bit.ly/2T47Ugb)

The edge is an uncomfortable place. It is more often than not sharp and pointy. It discombobulates us. It manifests as a murky tension between staying safe and moving towards something that contains elements of danger, mystery, and volatility. It can appear darker there, beyond the threshold. Upon arriving at the edge of our own threshold, our natural response is to shirk back and scramble for safety. Thar be monsters!

When what's right and what's safe are two different paths, your degree of willingness to be courageous is what determines the path you take. When what you truly want comes with uncertainty and risk, courage is your link between intention and action. To be a Change Maker, courage is your price of entry.

WHEN WHAT'S RIGHT AND WHAT'S SAFE ARE TWO DIFFERENT PATHS, YOUR DEGREE OF WILLINGNESS TO BE COURAGEOUS IS WHAT DETERMINES THE PATH YOU TAKE.

HOW TO GROW COURAGE

Do one thing every day that scares you.

ELEANOR ROOSEVELT

You're probably more courageous than you know. To get to where you are today, you've had to show courage. You learned to walk, right? That took courage. You already know how to be courageous. It's just about being more deliberate.

Here are some ways to develop and sustain your courage as a Change Maker.

1. Do a heat map.

It's often useful to remind yourself of when you've been courageous before, and what it took for you to be that way. You remind yourself of the 'courage toolkit' you already have.

One way to do this is to take an audit of your heat experiences – those times when you've faced a gnarly challenge, have been courageous, and leaned into it. These times can be powerful catalysts for learning and growth.

What have your heat experiences taught you? Use the following table to map your experiences and the lessons and principles they've taught you.

Experience	What I did that was courageous	What I learned about courage
Example: Meeting with General Manager	Called out his reluctance to confront poor performance	Speak my truth with compassion and clarity
1.		
2.		
3.		
4.		

Review the lessons. What are the themes for you here?

2. Be an experimentalist.

Failure is a mindset. And so is learning.

One of Leonardo Da Vinci's values was *dimostrazione*: a commitment to test knowledge through experience, persistence, and a willingness to learn from mistakes. He was someone who was always experimenting. And as a result, his legacy lives on today.

Often, the best way to get something to happen is to call it an experiment. A senior manager I used to work with got all sorts of things to happen in his corner of the organisation because he used to call them pilots. He'd say, "We're just going to pilot this for a few weeks and see what happens." Implicit in that message was the idea that it wasn't a permanent change – just trying something out. Of course, most of the pilots became a fixture. And for the ones that didn't? Well, they learned something anyway.

Making change actually isn't about making a big grandiose thing happen. It's about building something small, getting it to work, understanding why it works, and sharing that. And doing it again. And again. And again.

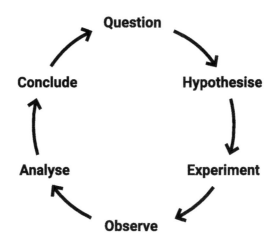

Be an experimentalist. Think like a scientist. Develop a hypothesis, and test it. Say:

If I try X, Y will happen. If Y happens then I'm one step closer to making change happen. If Z happens instead, well, I've learned something useful.

3. Treat courage as a practice.

Adults are more likely to act their way into a new way of thinking than to think their way into a new way of acting.

RICHARD PASCALE

When people face something big and scary, they'll often say, "I need to muster up the courage to tackle that."

Kind of like courage is something that's scattered around the place in small bits, and they just need to gather up all of those small bits and create a big courage ball. Then they'll be OK, and they can lean into the big thing and do what it takes.

Kind of like courage is something you need to draw on only occasionally. Like this:

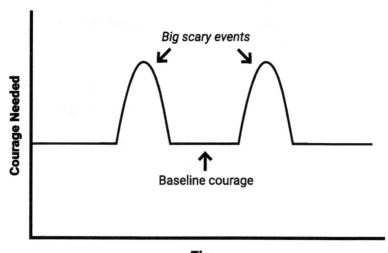

The rest of the time you just cruise.

You wish. Life doesn't work like that.

What if you viewed courage as a daily practice? Like going to the gym? Where you focus on building up your courage muscles so you can be ready to use them any time something scary comes across your radar. Like this:

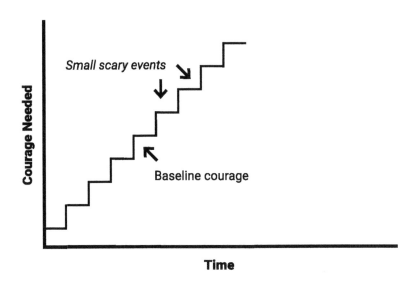

Daily living offers us heaps of opportunities to be courageous:

- Saying 'no' when you usually would say 'yes' (and vice-versa).
- Letting go of the need to control things so tightly.
- Approaching the person that makes you nervous.
- Speaking up and speaking out.
- Making a decision even when you don't have all the information.
- Letting someone know bad news.
- Challenging your story about what you believe life is all about.

When these sorts of challenges are thrown at us, we often let them go through to the keeper. If we do take them up, they can feel like hard work, and we shake in our boots. All because we haven't developed our courage muscles enough.

Develop your courage muscles through daily practice, and when the big gnarly ones come along, you'll be ready. The big decisions won't feel so big anymore.

So, what will it be today?

LEARN FASTER, GET CHANGE HAPPENING

Make fear a tailwind rather than a headwind.

JIMMY IOVINE

The mythologist Joseph Campbell said:

People say that what we're all seeking is a meaning for life. I don't think that's what we're really seeking. I think that what we're seeking is an experience of being alive.

You know from your own experience that the times when you've felt most alive, most 'on purpose', most energised, is when you've stepped up and out of your comfort zone. You've crossed a threshold from certainty to curiosity, from stability to dynamism. It's intoxicating. And it took courage.

Two main benefits of being that bit more courageous are **learning** and **progress.**

LEARNING

A mind stretched by a new experience can never go back to its old dimensions.

OLIVER WENDELL HOLMES

When you flex your courage muscles, you're creating the opportunity for new experiences. New experiences help you learn faster. When you learn faster, you're more quickly building a bigger base from which to act next time. And that means you can develop a broader perspective, more wisdom, and more confidence.

PROGRESS

When you act courageously, you're doing something differently. Doing something differently will likely get you a different outcome. Different outcomes create new insights, and opportunities for new doing. And the cycle continues.

What are you holding back from doing?

If you took decisive action, what would that say about who you are and what you stand for?

By not taking decisive action, what is it costing you?

Don't start with the second step. Start with the first. The step you don't want to take.

DAVID WHYTE, 'START CLOSE IN'

STEPPING UP

Amanda* is an up-and-coming leader in one of New Zealand's largest organisations, with a significant footprint offshore. When I met her, she was a participant on a leadership programme I was running. She was engaged, engaging, curious, and smart. Her presence radiated credibility and gravitas.

Amanda was preparing to go on her first leadership posting overseas. And she was terrified. It was the classic 'step up' scenario. She had excellent technical skills, and had a lot of the 'soft skills' that would make her an effective leader. But she'd never been in a people leadership role before, and this one was right at the 'pointy end'. She would not only be leading a team for the first time, she would also be running the whole office, while representing New Zealand in the country she was going to. The buck stopped with her.

Over the next 18 months, Amanda and I worked together in a coaching relationship. The first few months were rocky as she tried to find her feet. She'd adopted the mindset of a 'good soldier', trying to please everyone, including the team and her boss back in New Zealand, thinking this would deem her a 'success' in the eyes of others. She'd pass decisions up the line, or delay them. She'd avoid the difficult conversations. As a result, she was stretched in all directions and close to burnout. As a single mother of two, this was a significant challenge.

There came a turning point when she started to think about the impact she wanted to make before her posting was finished and she returned to New Zealand. What would be her legacy? At this point, she realised that unless she changed her mindset and behaviour, it wouldn't amount to much.

She decided on three priorities: 1) to leave the team in better shape than she found it; 2) to strengthen New Zealand's standing in that country; and 3) to build a reputation as an outstanding people leader.

With her conviction clear, her courage blossomed. She became less of a people pleaser. She hosted conversations with her team about the direction of the office, seeking input and setting clear priorities.

Name replaced to protect privacy

She invested in her people. She took less direction from head office and made more of the big calls herself. The icing on the cake was to initiate a series of conversations across leaders to reshape the organisation's policies to support single mothers working in the organisation's offshore locations.

She's since returned to New Zealand and continues to make waves, and is leading the charge in developing a policy for single mothers both in New Zealand and around the world.

CONCLUSION

We began this book with a few questions:

- How can I change how stuff gets done around here?
- How can I stay true to myself amidst the chaos?
- How can I learn to say no?
- How do I get traction and make my mark in this new role?
- How do I ensure I don't get stuck in the weeds, and keep a broader perspective?
- Where am I going in my career? How can I find the role or place that's 'me'?
- How can I reshape myself as an influential leader, not simply a technical expert?

How are you sitting with those questions now?

We also had a look at a few thoughts that might be rattling around in your head:

- I'm so frustrated right now. I feel like I'm going around in circles.
- I can see what needs to be done, but it's scary. I might fail.
- I feel like an imposter. Who am I to make this happen?
- If I want to be credible, I've got to show my expertise. Otherwise I'm a fake.
- It's not safe for me to be vulnerable or show my true colours in this culture/environment.
- Making change is too hard. It's easier to keep my head down and play it safe.

How have those thoughts changed for you now?

DESIRE VS FEAR

We all harbour two things:

1. A desire to be significant

....

2. Fear about our ability to be significant

....

These two things compete for our attention all the time. Which one do we listen to? The desire, or the fear?

Our desire to be significant is...significant. We want to be seen. We want to matter. As we've seen, the need for belonging and connection is a fundamental driver of the human motivation to act.

When we were younger, our strategies for being significant were relatively immature. We'd try to please others. We'd throw a tantrum to be heard. We'd try to control everything. Some of us hold onto these strategies well into adulthood, because these strategies work. They can give us a sense of security and we feel like we're seen. We matter.

The problem is, they're limited. Because they're driven by fear. A fear that if you're not seen, you don't matter. You're insignificant.

As we get older, most of us begin to rise above our insecurities and turn our attention outwards. How can I make a difference to others? How can I improve the world beyond myself? Our focus is on making a difference in the wider world. The desire for significance takes on new meaning.

The challenge is to make the desire bigger than the fear.

If we listen to the voice of fear, we'll amplify it. If we listen to our desire, that gets to play centre stage.

Which voice are you listening to?

GO FOR IT

Life is unfolding before you. The days, months, and years are flying by.

AND YOU ARE ALREADY MAKING AN IMPACT.

You can't *not*, remember?

The question is, is it the impact you want to make? Is desire trumping fear, or vice versa?

To make desire more powerful than fear, Change Makers cultivate four qualities:

Conviction: That's your fuel.

Curiosity: That keeps you learning.

Connection: That's your bridge to others.

Courage: That's what creates change.

These qualities give you strength. They help you dial up the music of desire and dial down the noise of fear. When you're strengthened by these qualities, life opens up. You make more waves. You have more fun. And you make the impact you know you are here to make.

Go for it.

....

YOU ARE ALREADY MAKING AN IMPACT.

RECOMMENDED READING

These books are ones I recommend every Change Maker reads. Of course, it's not an exhaustive list. Some of these I have referred to in this book, and others I've simply found incredibly useful to help me grow.

I've roughly categorised them into categories across the four C's, and have a 'catch all' list at the end.

CHANGING MAKING

How to Lead a Quest, by Jason Fox

Made to Stick, by Chip Heath and Dan Heath

Mastering Leadership, by Robert J. Anderson and William A. Adams

Mindset, by Dr. Carol S. Dweck

Rebel Talent, by Francesca Gino

The Art of Possibility, by Ben Zander and Rosamund Stone Zander

The Path of Least Resistance, by Robert Fritz

The Tipping Point, by Malcolm Gladwell

CONVICTION

Drive, by Daniel H. Pink

Good to Great, by Jim Collins

Man's Search for Meaning, by Viktor Frankl

So Good They Can't Ignore You, by Cal Newport

The Daily Stoic, by Ryan Holiday

The Hungry Spirit, by Charles Handy

The War of Art, by Steven Pressfield

CURIOSITY

21 Lessons for the 21st Century, by Yuval Noah Harari

Curious, by Ian Leslie

Cultivating Curiosity, by Evette Cordy

Don't Worry About the Robots, by Dr. Jo Cribb and David Glover

Immunity to Change, by Robert Kegan and Lisa Laskow Lahey

Leonardo Da Vinci, by Walter Isaacson

Originals, by Adam Grant

The Examined Life, by Stephen Grosz

The Hard Thing About Hard Things, by Ben Horowitz

COURAGE

Crossing the Unknown Sea, by David Whyte

Fierce Conversations, by Susan Scott

Mastery, by George Leonard

The Obstacle Is the Way, by Ryan Holiday

The Second Curve, by Charles Handy

CONNECTION

Antifragile, by Nassim Nicholas Taleb

Buddy System, by Geoffrey L. Greif

Feedback Flow, by Georgia Murch

Influence, by Robert Cialdini

It's Who You Know, by Janine Garner

Social: Why Our Brains Are Wired to Connect,
by Dr. Matthew Lieberman

This Is Marketing, by Seth Godin

Tribes, by Seth Godin

Work with Me, by Simon Dowling

What else are you reading? I'd love to hear. Drop me a line at **digby@digbyscott.com**

ABOUT THE AUTHOR

Digby Scott is a speaker, author, mentor, and facilitator who brings a fresh approach to leadership challenges. Creative, curious, and a master communicator, Digby has a unique perspective on the leadership and workplace challenges we are all trying to navigate.

He works best with 'restless go-getters' – those leaders and organisations that are on a mission to make a difference. His aim is to help people to think and act in new ways so that they nail it.

Digby has spent the last 20 years working in the leadership and organisational development fields. He's inspired thousands of leaders to learn how to develop themselves, and grow others, so they create lives worth living and cultures worth being a part of.

As a former Chartered Accountant with a Big Four firm, and having led and sold numerous businesses, Digby understands the commercial realities leaders face. He's also been the President of the International Coaching Federation's Western Australian chapter, and has coached well over 1000 leaders. Working with Digby, you get to benefit from all of this experience.

For more information
about Digby's work
and thinking, visit
digbyscott.com